THE INVENTION OF EXPRESSIONISM

MAX RAPHAEL

THE INVENTION OF EXPRESSIONISM

CRITICAL WRITINGS 1910–1913

EDITED AND TRANSLATED BY PATRICK HEALY

WITH JOHN CONOLLY AND BRENDAN O'BYRNE

NOVEMBER EDITIONS
MMXVI

Copyright © 2016 by November Editions & Patrick Healy

Design and layout: The Curved House

All rights reserved. This book or any portion thereof
may not be reproduced or used in any manner whatsoever
without the express written permission of the publisher
except for the use of brief quotations in a book review.

ISBN 978-94-92027-09-2

November Editions – Amsterdam

For more information on our publications,
feel free to contact us at:

hello@novembereditions.com

www.NovemberEditions.com

CONTENTS

INTRODUCTION: MAX RAPHAEL AND
THE INVENTION OF EXPRESSIONISM 1

CRITICAL WRITINGS 1910–1913

THE AMERICAN EXHIBITION 43

BERLIN EXHIBITIONS 50

A BOOK ON MANET 57

THE SONDERBUND IN DÜSSELDORF 59

BERLIN, WORLD CITY 66

OSSIP DYMOW: THE YOUNGSTER VLAS 72

THE NEW SECESSION 74

WHITE AND BLACK 78

THE ACADEMY AND THE NEW ARTISTS'
ASSOCIATION 85

CURT HERMANN: THE STRUGGLE FOR STYLE 88

THE NEW SECESSION 90

THE NEW PAINTING. THE NEW SECESSION 96

THE 'NEW SECESSION' IN BERLIN 104

LIEBERMANN'S GOOD SAMARITAN 107

EXPRESSIONISM 113

HENRI BERGSON'S WRITINGS 122

PAINTING AND PERSONALITY 129

GOETHE'S BIRTHDAY IN WEIMAR 139

PURRMANN AND LEVY 143

BERLIN EXHIBITIONS 147

ON MODERN PAINTING 156

CHARLES DE COSTER, FLEMISH LEGENDS 159

DEAR MR PECHSTEIN! 161

MAX PECHSTEIN 165

BIBLIOGRAPHY: THE EARLY CRITICAL WRITINGS OF
MAX RAPHAEL (1910–1913) 171

ACKNOWLEDGEMENTS 175

INTRODUCTION

MAX RAPHAEL AND THE INVENTION OF EXPRESSIONISM

The following publication is an artificial construct. It is concerned with Expressionism as it developed and was defined in Berlin around the years 1910-11. It takes a small section of the lifetime of research by Max Raphael and places his early articles and reviews under the rubric 'The Invention of Expressionism'. All of the texts which are translated here appeared in German and under the pseudonym Schönlanke or Schönlank, after the town where Raphael was born on the 27th of August 1889 (initially Max Raphael Schönlanke, and thereafter M.R. Schönlank).

Schönlanke was a small border town in the then Prussian province of Posen. Raphael lived here for the first ten years of his life and then moved to Berlin, where he lived with his grandparents. His father had hoped Raphael would study law, but he was to begin his academic life at the University of Munich in 1907, then followed courses in Berlin, and later returned to Munich again to study under, among others, Heinrich Wölfflin, who had already developed his immensely influential theory on the principles of art history. When Wölfflin rejected Raphael's proposal to write a thesis on Picasso, Raphael set out on his travels and independent career, eventually attending lectures under the philosopher Georg Simmel in Berlin. Some of the details of these early years can be found in a manuscript entitled "Biographie", which has not yet been published.[1]

A remarkable feature of Raphael's life was the independence of his study of contemporary artistic trends and personalities. The article "Der Expressionismus" of 1911 is the first with such a title in the German language, and effectively signalled the revolt of a young generation in Berlin against the world of their parents. It should also be mentioned that, in 1913, Raphael published the first book which had the name Picasso on the title page: *Von Monet zu Picasso*.[2]

Raphael is in his early 20s as he struggles with the tendencies and events in Berlin of which he is one of the most significant witnesses. The nature of the city, the revolt of the young (most of the artists about whom he is writing are of his own age), and the pathos of anti-bourgeois militancy of those whom he spoke of as 'refugees in this age' bear testimony to his growing awareness and stringent advocacy of the newest in life and art that the city offered.

Reading the articles in mostly chronological sequence gives one a ringside seat to the various movements and currents of artistic influence and action in Berlin in the pre-WWI decades. It is exciting and unsettling, and has as much the brilliance of an invention as the travails of a birth. The intense welcoming of the modern, and the sense that a new epoch was in the making is reflected in all of the pieces. Raphael would remark, as a defender of the latest artistic movement:

'the young too are on their way to art.' Theirs was a way, he maintained, different to that of the Impressionists, but with the same vitality and artistry.

At the age of 21 Raphael left his studies in Munich. He would spend the rest of his life engaged in research and writing as an independent scholar, with one short period of teaching, and would leave a legacy of writing on art which has had few equals in the 20th century. The clearest account available in English is still *The Demands of Art*, edited by Herbert Read and Robert Cohen, and translated by Norbert Guterman. The inclusion in that volume of the essay "Towards an Empirical Theory of Art", which Raphael wrote whilst crossing from Europe to America, fleeing Nazi persecution, remains indispensable for understanding his singular achievements.[3]

The long trajectory of Raphael's engagement starts with the articles and reviews included here. They allow one to begin the intricate and delicate task of reconstructing his intellectual development. The texts show how Raphael starts to come to terms with Impressionism and its impact on Germany, to distinguish the new tendencies in German art from the older generation – Liebermann and Corinth – and align himself with an adumbration of the distinctions in what he would name 'der Expressionismus', arguing that it was not 'primitive' in the derogatory sense with which it had been first maligned. From this early work one can track major concerns of Raphael throughout his life. However, the present publication confines itself to a small section of his original and compelling achievements, which can be followed in relatively precise detail from the day he left Munich until the last year before the outbreak of the First World War.

By 1909 Raphael decided to leave Munich and enrol as a student of philosophy in Berlin. In 1910 there is a trip to Italy, where he first sees the art of Giotto and Tintoretto, and visits Ravenna. He describes the encounters as among the most meaningful for his later work. Furthermore, it is essentially the meeting with the painter Max Pechstein that brings him into the major artistic movements taking place in Berlin. The year is summarised as follows: 'Encounter with Pechstein (and his generation). Journey to Holland and wandering along the Rhine. First encounter with French art. Decision to travel to Paris. Platonic relationship to Anka (Waiting in the evening for her to come from work).[4]

Five articles appear under pseudonym that year: an article on an exhibition of American art in the Academy; a review of several Berlin exhibitions; a review of a book on Manet; an account of the Sonderbund in Düsseldorf, and a review of Scheffler's book *Berlin*. He continues to write under a pseudonym until 1913, when his first book-length study – *Von Monet zu Picasso* – is published, a work which seems to have been in preparation since late 1910.[5] The articles situate Raphael's many-sided involvements and give us the beginning of his allegiances and tastes at this date. In the first article to appear, "The American Exhibition", Raphael proposes a theme of universal history in considering its course follows the path of the sun. He remarks: 'Even the sober academic brain can point out connections between the course of the sun and the path of culture.' The image is directly taken from Hegel, although Raphael gives Oscar Wilde as his source. The instinct for grand theory is fully alive in this early publication, and it expresses much of the 'historicist' effusion such as culminates in the work of Spengler:

> If we use a globe to put our historical knowledge in order, then we begin right in the East, with China, from where our thoughts move on to India and Persia; and from there to Egypt, on the one hand, and to Greece (by way of Asia Minor), Italy and France on the other. Here the ocean checks the flight of our thoughts; a new world begins on the other side, the western hemisphere: America, the west coast of which, like our starting point, is washed by the Pacific Ocean. Picking up Japan, we complete our circle, with its end placed beside its beginning. To be sure I have used an analogy to anticipate my conclusion.[6]

The conclusion is that the new forms of art, democratic and economically based, will come from America. The geographic analogy requires a specific territory, the area between the Northern Tropic and the Arctic Circle, between the thirtieth and fiftieth parallel. To the North one can ascribe the rigid, cold and doubt filled aspects of cultural development, and instincts, feeling and belief to the South.

To understand the symbol of the circle of history, Raphael introduces another figure, which gives a function to the individual period that makes up the whole, namely the spiral: 'It is the spiral, almost closing in a circle, winding inwards in parallel curves, and then outward in a similar movement, from an inmost point, it is this line which symbolises the event.'[7] What the number of spirals have been is impossible to tell; all one can say is that they are similar with respect to content – if one abstracts the content sufficiently – and Raphael then argues that in the course of events it is forms, not contents that change. Form is the new, and in every single period a form is perfected, becomes the model, and it does so mostly at the expense of others. Periods flow into each other and contemporary historical science recognises that each period has its corresponding form of art.

The complex metaphor is disrupted by Raphael's analysis of the character of the current practise of art, which he sees as aristocratic and reactionary, defending itself against the new form of democratisation, that of economic life and all art deriving from it:

> Everywhere art lies under the false influence of science, or gives off the delicate rotting odour of our sublimest Impressionists and sentimental poetasters. In its lonely hiding place behind the confusion of books and pictures, made for the very few who have developed their senses most exquisitely, we find art for art's sake; purposeless art, useless art, the only art of our time.[8]

It is the decaying aristocracy still there in every area: Monet, Stefan George, Nietzsche. But the American exhibition only displays itself as a variation on French art: 'pictures created from European influences, which only demonstrate national character in the appreciation and exploitation of impressions, that is to say in the choice of models and in their transformations. Here we see the upper limits of their artistic powers, which are too weak for autonomous, primary creation.'[9] The basic content is the same as in Europe: portrait, interior, landscape. Raphael notes that it is landscape 'which is the mother of our modern painting', and that in this area the French of the older and newer schools have produced the best. The Americans have obviously followed the Barbizon masters, followed by Monet and the Impressionists.

Whilst noting the influence and dependency, Raphael hesitates to define Impressionism: 'In spite of all the confusion of ideas I cannot define the essence of French Impressionism at this point.'[10] With the exception of Whistler, the Americans are only the equivalent of run-of-the mill French artists. Raphael sees strength in the American rejection of the western European art of decadence, which is in the long view only an expression of the death-knell of the Christian era first sounded in the collapse of the *ancien régime* in the French Revolution. He approvingly cites a work by Jensen on 'New Machines' in which the domestic architecture of the Americans is seen as determined by use value, before any thinking about architecture: 'One will see later that this style is beautiful. For beauty follows truth, as it does strength.'[11]

In the examination of the Berlin exhibitions which appeared in the journal *März* in August of 1910, Raphael begins to provide his definition of art, without 'of course' characterising Impressionism. His starting point is the assertion that anyone who has ever become truly conscious of his surroundings and his own self will experience a shock in the chaotic confusion of phenomena and try to overcome it. This idea of *Shock-Erlebnis* is directly derived from Simmel (whose lectures Raphael attended in Berlin) in his essay on "The Metropolis and Mental Life", and indeed continues to have, down to the late work of Benjamin, considerable impact on the characterising of modernity in the urban setting.[12] Raphael argues that art can be defined as the shaping of this chaotic play through art's specific means. He draws his definition explicitly from Emile Zola, and thinks it the 'most comprehensive of our time', namely that a work of art is 'a corner of nature viewed through a temperament', a direct quotation from Zola's *Mes haines* of 1886.

Raphael emphasises that it is the temperament that is the determining factor in art. The conclusion follows that there can be as many works of art as there are individuals, a definition so wide one ends up with an almost 'nihilistic plethora of possibilities'. Close observation makes differentiation of temperament visible. Raphael illustrates this with the examples of Wilhelm Trübner and Max Liebermann: 'Although they share a virile energy one begins to detect nuances in their techniques; this is the handwriting of character. Trübner places his dots cleanly side by side. When one is close up to the canvas one can enjoy the pleasure of the artist in the purity of beautiful matter and its beautiful purposeful positioning.' His work gives us the whole force, the brutality even of the real phenomenon. There is in this work a painter's love of the powerful tones of colour which approach the strength of those in nature, and Raphael suggests one loves this being drunk with decorative colour, the tonal beauty, and the means having no purpose but themselves.[13]

The contrast with Liebermann is drawn. Up close Liebermann's canvas is a messy palette, with a thin, jagged, nervous stroke. But when you step back the surfaces acquire form and spatial relationships to one another: 'Then space begins to sing and sound unexpected melodies, and in a state of puzzlement, you ask: How?' There is a wealth of exactness in the tonal gradation. The entire colour is a means necessary for the formation of the whole. The temperament of these artists is that of a delicate sensibility which reacts to external impressions with undreamt of sharpness. There is a sense from the pictures that the artist feels the whole weight of the subjective self, and at the same time, given the feeling of relativity which decentres man as the meaning of existence, there is an unsureness and insecurity:

> Appropriate to the delicacy of sensibility we see a profound penetration of nature, a discovery of her charms, which are so new and various that one has not recognised them in their full depth, in Cézanne for example. The effect of relativity is to arrange the objects in a living sensuous atmosphere, to take from them their individual charms, and thus neutralise them so that they become passive, accepting, and just like the creating subject. Arising from this unsure and forced knowledge is a grotesque element that I sense just as much in the piety and reverence of Monet as I do in the sharpness and abstraction of Liebermann.[14]

The effect of this is a return to observation, which Raphael sees as, the 'fundamental value of this school which has developed a general idea of style from the naturalistic representation of phenomena.'[15]

What is of deeper interest to Raphael in the article "Berlin Exhibitions", is the way the artists have occupied themselves with history painting. Unlike Liebermann's Samson and Delilah, which was exhibited in 1903, the current younger artists go to the work with a different spirit. Slevogt, in his canvas The Hörselberg, 'has completely fallen victim to the greater danger of picturesque composition.' Raphael reserves his best appreciation for Beckmann's work on show, The Dispensation of the Holy Ghost: 'Beckman is more fortunate,' – than Slevogt that is – 'his warring colours give us something of the visionary nature of the subject.' However, none of these works would compare favourably with the achievements of the cartoons by Puvis de Chavannes included in the exhibition. Yet, Raphael argues that with patient work the 'Hotspurs of today' can achieve the status of acknowledged masters. He sees them as pathfinders and leaders with strong will, a will to transform nature, where their objects are the gods:

> And what of will? This ego that has no trust in fate? This individual who is neither willing nor able to lose himself in nature, who must rather dominate it? This is what the Romantics ask. Here, too, these opponents of the imperative of the day seem to produce as many works of art as there are individuals. They, however, derive their rules from themselves and not from the objects.

Raphael also points to a limitation of such a will in the work of Hofmann and Hodler, especially the 'will to beauty' in Hofmann, in whose frescoes in the Weimar Theatre, for example, means can become an end in themselves and atrophy into the decorative.[16]

The other important aspect of young artists' work today is that they wish to form the laws of the spatial 'not out of the object, not out of themselves, but out of the wall and its mood. A decoration must be formed from the play of closed colour surfaces and lines. Here, perhaps, we find a difference in principle that has led to the founding of the New Secession.'[17] Raphael identifies Pechstein as the strongest temperament and concludes: 'we must wait to see what he brings us.'

In the short review of Theodore Duret's *Life of Manet*, we see that Raphael gains a clearer understanding of Manet's social milieu and the psychology of the public. Even though Raphael cannot find a precise exposition of Manet's style in Duret's book, he calls it an able contribution to the understanding of Impressionism that, with its carefully chosen photographs and etchings and well-reproduced drawings, 'convey[s] to us the immediate feeling of Manet's hand and the shiver of creation'.[18]

In what is the most significant review from this year, that of the Sonderbund exhibition in Düsseldorf, Raphael turns to the question of what distinguishes the current work of the young from that of the Impressionists. This exhibition, which was hosted in the city from July 16 to October 9, also showcased the latest developments in French painting, and Raphael sees it as being set up to make a comparison with Impressionism, 'an undertaking of an extent hitherto unknown in Germany'. He sets out to provide an explanation and clarification of the principles stimulated by the sharp confrontation 'between two movements in art':

> Impressionism is a personal attitude to the cosmos, one which creates by following nature, and this by the emphasis placed on the moving elements of light and air, by a character of deeply penetrating feeling and sensitivity. Impressionism, thus restricted in the type of artist and constrained in its choice of object, has been able to create a style. Its narrow compass of the landscape has given it a general subject matter, something which all good and fruitful artistic ages have provided for themselves. (…) The impression can be a double one. Firstly a sensation of the momentary in which only the life of the instant is to be found. In this case one shows one's personality through the number of moments perceived and expressed (…) Then we have a sensation of the momentary that is

a variation on the general, an expression of that instant that is nevertheless the whole soul of the landscape. One could speak of the impression of the inward. Here the personality will reveal itself to the degree in which its empathy has raised the invisible heart of the landscape to life in each of its momentary transformations. In the first case, Impressionism is more an international, and in the second case more a national mode of expression.[19]

On the basis of that distinction Raphael then notes how the Germans have been completely international, although the not very mobile character of their vision would demand a completely national approach. However, he also sees they have been forced into this international style because, he suggests, the German landscape is generally 'too hard in its atmosphere, too immovable, and when mobile too hidden, too difficult to catch'.

The result of course is that, all in all, the Impressionist movement has foundered in Germany, the truth of which, he says, one can see for oneself in Düsseldorf. The example to support this judgement is given in the work of Julius Bretz, who Raphael notes displays something of the idiosyncrasy of the Lower Rhine, 'something of the melancholy of the plain and its loneliness, the loneliness with which a white house stands out against a green tree and blue shadows fall on the whitewash, and in the curve of the region's hills.'[20] However, it is clear that Bretz is not an Impressionist, his emphasis being nearly always on the enduring, 'and thus he works with line'. Alterations caused by movements are to him more a stimulus to mood than phenomena to be studied with the eye. Even the self-proclaimed Impressionist Clarenbach cannot produce the character of the Lower Rhine. These artists have an excess of technical means, too little to say, and are smug, lacking either unashamed honesty or sufficient diligence.

Liebermann is a different case: 'one can easily assign to him his place among the Impressionists. What characterises him is his feeling for space, for monumental line, which has a slightly grotesque effect, and for bodily movement. The painterly means which produce this are more colourist than tonal. He conquers colour hue by hue, but in such a way that each is judged against a fine shade of grey that he finds at the seashore at certain times, at certain levels of the tide.'[21]

It is here, with respect to colour, that Raphael sees what the new breakthrough is for artists. Looking at the French school represented at the Sonderbund, he comments directly on Vuillard that he 'produces a sensitive impression of total mood by areas of thin colour on a ground which has also become part of the effect.' Signac, represented in the show by three pictures, 'brings the splitting up of colour to its highest pitch. He places his dots of blue, red, green and yellow side by side like tesserae so that, through their contrasting play of mood, he can reproduce the air and light of nature with increased distinctness. One has come from nature and finally arrives through technical means at decoration'.[22]

Even if the work reminds Raphael of the mosaics at Ravenna, which he had seen the previous year, he notices how, in the case of Signac, the mosaics' linear contour is absent, and 'everything must be synthesised by the viewer'; however, 'going back a certain distance, nature recaptures its objective forms, the pattern of dots can no longer defy synthesis.'

The new painting has been consciously flat, decoratively so, from the very beginning, a decoration achieved through insights into colour attained by the Impressionists. By this I mean that nature has lost every objective value and that the artist's imagination, working as it does with colours, has now won for itself a limitless, unbridled freedom.[23]

Raphael quotes from the foreword to the exhibition catalogue written by Dr. Niemeyer, an art historian who had taught at the Düsseldorf *Kunstgewerbeschule* since 1905, and who was keenly interested in the relation of arts and crafts and the relationship between German and French art. The 1910 exhibition was held in the Kunstpalast, with 242 exhibits of painting and sculpture and a larger number of *objets d'art*, and did not go on tour. Its theme was precisely stated in the foreword: *Deutsche und französische Neukunst*.[24]

Niemeyer argues for the place of Cézanne (not exhibited at the show), who 'through sculptural structure and the simplification of form reacted against the subtle optical analysis of phenomena of the clear, more northerly manner of Impressionism.' Matisse had recently gained influence by enacting the linear essence from Cézanne's sculptural constructions:

His (Matisse's) pictures too have the effect of classical examples of the type. The picture is no longer an abundance of seemingly arbitrarily positioned points or specks of colour, but divided up into two or three large colour surfaces. The artistic power is expressed in the rhythm in which areas reciprocate each other and in which bodies are placed on these surfaces; then in the balancing of colours, which must have a particular ring, since they have to be seen in large areas. One wants to have form, but not that of nature. One wants rather the subjectively decorative, hence the line is neither formation, formative, nor an expression of form, but a decorative outline or inline which betrays the artist's character by its curves.[25]

Raphael offers a critical and crucial comparison between the work Matisse and that of Kandinsky:

We can see how much more can be got out of this by comparing the pictures of Kandinsky (Munich) with the dry sobriety of Matisse. Kandinsky's works seek the personal expression of a personal mood in a coloured composition. So he calls out full speed ahead with his shades of green, blue, red and ochre. (…) One is always looking for chances to make comparisons with nature; one's meagre training is for this. Here one's model has completely disappeared. The artist no longer receives his laws from the object; the mirror of his imagination is everything. Science and imitation making have vanished again in favour of making anew. One would certainly wish that these new pictures would be hung in a new way also, i.e. appropriate to their inner demand. They belong not in a frame on the wall, but without a frame in the wall.[26]

Once again it seems that Pechstein is the source for introducing Raphael to the work of Matisse, which he may have first encountered at this exhibition. Pechstein had a studio in Paris and met Matisse there during a six month stay in 1908. His influence on Pechstein becomes especially evident from 1911–12.

Unlike Raphael, Walter Cohen's review of the exhibition – which appeared in *Kunstchronik* on October 28 of 1910 – praised the hanging of the show, and made the point that many of the painters from France appeared for the first time in Germany: Vlaminck, Braque, Dérain, Friesz, Guerin. The Matisse's on show came from the Folkwang Museum in Essen.

It is appropriate that Raphael concluded his year of publishing with a long essay review on Scheffler' book Berlin, in which Raphael intertwines his own understanding of the city. Some of the points he makes are directly Simellian, and in others he has both a wider historical view and suggestions about the way of writing which are indicative of a shift in his understanding towards the city of his adoption with which he increasingly becomes involved. Initially he makes the point that there is an inward migration to Berlin from the East. The change in population and size of the city is a matter not just of quantity but of quality: 'One will be at first increasingly astonished by the increase in numbers and dimensions (…) One first learns to recognise and love the novelties of a great metropolis in what is visible, palpable, in the changes in the streetscape.'[27]

In his *Expressionism: Art and Idea* (1987), Donald E. Gordon argues the now standard view that it was in the years 1910-11 in Berlin that a unified Expressionist movement was born. Gordon argues for the importance of the New Secession in helping to bring this about, because not only did it bring the provincial Brücke group to sudden national attention, with its woodcuts regularly produced in *Der Sturm* in the course of 1911, but it also brought Dresden, Berlin, Munich and Prague Expressionists together as early as November of 1911. Gordon identifies the author of the exhibition catalogue correctly as

Max Raphael and is the first to note Raphael's significance in relation to the development of this movement, without however being aware that he also published the first article with the title "Der Expressionismus".[28]

> As Raphael wrote in the catalogue of its third exhibition, Neue Secession art was an expressive art of 'decoration'. "(T)he young artists of all countries (…) no longer take their rules from the object, whose impression impressionists tried to reach with the means of pure painting, instead they think of the wall and for the wall, purely in colours. They no longer want to reproduce nature in each of its transient manifestations. Rather they condense their personal sensations of an object, then compress them into a characteristic expression, in such a way that the expression of personal sensations is strong enough to produce a wall painting. A coloured decoration."

Gordon comments on this extract he provides: 'But Raphael's remarks describe as much a Fauve as a Post-Impressionist point of view. And the art of such prominent New Secession exhibitors as César Klein, Georg Taffert and Lasar Segal would readily fit this generic description. Still it is the New Secession leader Max Pechstein, who had extensive experiences with decorative wall painting and even stained glass windows, to whom Raphael's words most directly apply.'[29]

The New Secession show to which the catalogue by Raphael refers ran from February to April 1911, and indeed did have many of the artists who would later be identified by him as Expressionists, such as Heckel, Kirchner, Klein, Melzer, Mueller, Nolde, Pechstein, Schmidt-Rotluff, Segal and Taffert.

Indeed it was clear, as Cohen had noted in his review of the Sonderbund, that the influence of Van Gogh on Nolde, and of Nolde on Berlin, along with the increasing awareness of the Fauves, including Gauguin, was impacting in Berlin in a direct way. Nolde remains an extraordinary and strange figure in all of this, being not only the oldest of the 'young generation', already in his 40s, but also expressing a view that belonged more to the Kaiser and his court than to his fellow artists. In his own autobiographical writing, for example, Nolde reports how he 'was tortured by not knowing whether Cubism and Constructivism were created by Jews, and originated in the Jewish mentality.'[30]

What of course becomes clear in this period from October 1910 to September 1911, is the awareness of how much the art practise of the city of Berlin was detested by the official culture. In his work on *Weimar Culture*, Peter Gay takes this hostility as a given of the imperial policy, whose own urge for monumentality could be seen in the kitsch decoration of the *Siegessäulle* in the Tiergarten. The Kaiser's known hostility to and interference in the art world is best seen in the dismissal of Tschudi from the National Gallery. This episode was significant in that it drew the lines between official and unofficial art.[31]

The most astonishing developments in 1911 can all be gathered around Raphael's encounter in the spring with a single work of Picasso. It is as dramatic an encounter as one can imagine, and registered by Raphael as fatidic. There is a letter from New York dated 1943 in which he recalls that day in Paris and puzzles over the enduring fascination of Picasso, and indeed Matisse and Braque, noting that, even given the shifts in his thinking afterwards, he realises that they were the ones who have remained and will endure; they have painted 'immortality', and thereby silenced critique.

Raphael's article "Reminiscence of Picasso", written in 1931 during a recuperation from a lung illness in Davos[32] tells the story simply, and in its conclusion there is a kind of melancholic charm. Straying from the grand boulevards on an early spring day in 1911, Raphael walked into an unknown side-street. In a show window he saw a small painting that struck him forcibly as something completely new, and the fulfilment of the deepest wishes. He only realised how long he had been standing staring from the gestures of people who started to stare at him and mutter remarks. He asked to be shown another picture, but was asked to return the next day and so on for weeks, without another being produced; rather he was shown an album with photographs of works. One day two men came into the shop and, after an ironic remark of the dealer, one of them turned around and looked at Raphael intently: 'Would you like to come and visit my atelier?' He wrote the address on his *carte de visite*. 'That is incredible,' said the dealer, 'Picasso has just given you the address of his atelier, to which no one is invited.'

Picasso's atelier was almost empty, with white walls, and just a pipe rack hanging there. There was possibly a rickety red plush chair with a dodgy leg, and so they both sat on the ground before the easel, on which there was a small, minutely executed picture. Raphael recalls that never before nor afterwards had he the impression in an atelier of being, as here, in a medieval monk's cell. Picasso certainly didn't have the physical build of a monk, but in his speaking there was a sense of the loner. There were scraps of sentences from a monologue that perhaps no one but himself, or maybe Braque, understood, which had been going on for a year. This is the beginning of the fateful meeting as recounted later.[33]

In the "Biographie" the whole year 1911 is characterised by the 'first trip to Paris, meeting with Picasso (and Cézanne collection), Matisse.'[34]

Raphael's writing on the third New Secession also meant he had 'arrived' in the complex art world of Berlin. Peter Paret leaves no doubt in his book-length study *The Berlin Secession* that the history of the Berlin Secession is the history of Germany's encounter with modernism. Paret also argues of the view that the German variety of Impressionism never achieved a level of originality to make a lasting impact on international taste. Unlike the Munich and Vienna Secessions, Berlin enjoyed no official support, at least not for the first twelve years of its existence. The opening show of the Berlin Secession had constituted the first major battle about Impressionism in Germany, in the summer of 1898.

Paret takes the view that, given the strict State patronage of Wilhemine Prussia, this exhibition – with its annihilation of a realistic picture of the world, the assertion of instability and ambiguity, its international character – constituted and was seen as a fundamental threat to the art policy of Prussia. Unlike Vienna, the Berlin Secession faced actual hostile political powers. The position of the Cassirer gallery was also unusual in that no art dealer, not even in Vienna, specialised in modern French art. He shows however a change in the position of the Secession when from 1910 it had begun to receive official prizes.[35]

The article by Raphael is really his taking sides in the increasingly acrimonious politics of the burgeoning Berlin scene. It is likely that Pechstein had gained him the commission to write for the exhibition. Although circumstances were so volatile Pechstein left the group, and was expelled from the Brücke in the same year. He was considered a tyrant.

Many other elements were now in the explosive brew: Oskar Kokoschka from Vienna was being championed by Herwarth Walden, whose journal *Der Sturm* had been launched in March 1910; the official interference with the production of the works of Strauss; the appearance in February 1911 of Pfemfert's *Die Aktion*, the radical pacifist, anarchic journal which also engaged in art politics directly.

Raphael had gone to Paris and whilst there attended lectures of Bergson, on whom he published two articles in 1911. These articles open up Raphael's theoretical position in the most explicit way, in that they show his 'spiritualist' influence from Bergson, or directly his anti-positivist stance, which one can see in his reading of Mach, and also alert one to his interest in the 'psychology' of creation. Bergson had lectured mainly on James in that year. Raphael also attended the lectures of Emile Mâle, the great scholar of medieval French iconography, whose work on medieval French art remains a milestone of art historical scholarship. It is the article "Painting and Personality", published in *Die Aktion*, that lets one see where Raphael is standing in his own thinking.

The month of February saw not only the launch of *Die Aktion*, but also the opening of the third exhibition of the New Secession in Berlin's Maximilian Mach Gallery. In the foreword to the catalogue, Raphael gives his developed understanding of the artistic aims of his generation with greater precision than at the end of the previous year. The issues with regard to Impressionism have been clarified for him: it had been a psychology of nature which had left the studio and gone to nature, an art that was hungry to capture the delights of air and light in colours. It was the need to capture the impression of every moment, each hour, even the temperature. Therefore the very need to fix every visible value on the picture surface also meant that the 'decorative elements were greatly neglected'. Raphael offers a clear summary of the newest tendencies in art:

> A decoration achieved through the colour-perceptions of Impressionism: that is the programme of every country's young artists, i.e. they no longer get their laws from the object. The Impressionists had wished to achieve the impression of the object by means of pure painting; these latter, however, thought of the wall and for the wall and indeed in colours. No longer did they want to reproduce nature in her evanescent appearances, but rather to so concentrate their personal feelings towards the object, compressing them into a characteristic expression, that the expression of their personal feelings is strong enough to become a mural.[36]

Raphael places the new requirement in a short phrase which he will then elaborate, and which explains the difference with the research of the Impressionists:

> For a colourful decoration. One places areas of colour side by side, so that these incalculable laws of quantitative colour equilibrium, together with a new freedom of

action, will abrogate the rigid scientific laws of qualitative colour. These colour areas do not destroy the basic lines of the represented objects; rather the line is now consciously used as a factor, not expressive of form, not modelling, but descriptive of form, expressing sensation and pinning figural life to the surface. The mere fixing of everything to the surface entirely cancels its significance as reality. Each and every object is just the bearer of a colour, a composition of colours, and the whole work is aimed at the impression not of nature, but of sensations.'[37]

He then alludes to the politics of the Secession: 'last summer led to an unavoidable split in the Secession. The best of the young artists, the hopeful bearers of a future that is capable of development, have formed themselves into a new Secession.'[38] Raphael makes the startling criticism of the very dubious efforts to exhibit these artists, in spaces that resembled the artificial temperature of greenhouse cultivation, and continues: 'one wrapped the young artists in lovely flattering words, in expressions of praise such as 'talent' or 'genius', always hung the worst of the works sent in, or displayed them dreadfully or ripped the coherence of the collection to pieces until one turned them all down. The mutually contradictory introductions of the last two catalogues form a clear expression of their behaviour towards the young artists. One speaks of their puerile technique, the other of promising talent. One speaks of rebels, the other of artists spoiled to the point of modishness.'

Raphael draws his attention to a different analysis, not any longer of the true and beautiful or the ideals of the 'aesthetic', but focussing instead on the creative nature in man, which comes into existence as soon as he has secured his day to day life: 'Now this characteristic art is the only true one. If it produces its effect from the inward, unified, personal independent feeling, unconcerned with, indeed unconscious of, everything outside, be it born of the wildest crudity or the most cultivated sensibility, it will be whole ad living.'

Raphael repeats much of the catalogue text in an article, again under the title of "The 'New Secession' in Berlin", published the magazine *Bildende Kunstler* probably in April. It condenses the views expressed in the original catalogue and adds some new observations. The problem of the neglect of the decorative element of the picture is now seen as caused by the instance of separation between perception and reaction. The real gains of Impressionism were not in the works themselves, but 'in the new colour-scale abstracted from its rendering of nature.'

In this account Raphael also cites again the historical development as posited by Niemeyer, who had organised the Sonderbund in Düsseldorf: 'Impressionism was superseded by the style of Cézanne, the logical extension of Manet's optical synthesis, which after the atmospherical absolutism of landscape art once again taught one to understand painting as the pure creation of colour. Cézanne's art represented the new generation with the problem of conglomerating the inconceivable sum of the optical faces of nature into colour surfaces which are clear and simple and suffused with the breath of the most delicate contrasts, of comprehending the functional unity of bodily appearance.'

Raphael repeats almost exactly the citation which he used in the Sonderbund exhibition review, and thus this article collates two earlier pieces, suggesting something of the speed with which he was working during this year. It adds however a list of names for the generalised 'young generation', and explains that it is not just one tendency alone that is shown. Thus again referring to the split, he says that the 'group of evicted artists does not only consist in the representatives of the new thoughts on style such as Pechstein, Kirchner, Schmidt-Rotluff, Nolde and Heckel. The chance circumstances of its formation have brought two lyricists into the circle, Melzer and Müller-Steglitz; these circumstances have also made the New Secession into the collecting point for young artists in general, into the place where every young potential will find a welcome.'

In a third article on the New Secession, Raphael sets out what seems increasingly to be his settled opinion and emphatically takes sides with the younger artists. Here he takes the conflict between the 'old' and the New Secession, which he has previously reported on in a summary fashion, to be a necessary one, and argues that the new generation behind these works is another artistic type. He also sets himself the task of writing about this type, so that one could achieve a positive attitude towards pictures that have been ridiculed beyond measure.

In his short review of Ossip Dymow's *The Youngster Vlas* of the preceding year, Raphael had made a slanting reference to the characteristics of the new generation. In "Berlin, World-City" he had also tried to capture something of the types coming into being, the Berliner, and what this signified for a future. The reference to Dymow:

> His is an extraordinary gift, and the scenes, especially those at the end, become very alive (…). I have long been interested in this material. When Dymow has the

youngster Vlas grow up, he does not present us with the psychology of an adult but rather with the modern child, the inherited nervousness, the awe of everything marvellous and mysterious, an image of the cold, analytic physiological scepticism of those born around 1890, the fruit of the generation of Ibsen Maeterlinck and Marx.[39]

This is also the generation to which Raphael himself belongs. He adds a further coda to that description of Vlas, and extends it to the current context in Berlin:

> The new generation is the heir of the older. That which an unfettered individualism has created and conquered with an astonishing fecundity and rich confusion will have to be taken up again and re-experienced in this total breadth by them, in order to try and shape a new life from it.

In an appeal as much as an analysis, Raphael suggests that if development is to be at all possible, the following generation has to take this burden upon itself joyfully, 'to affirm it exultantly' and he notes that:

> [I]n every area of intellectual activity the mask of the generation is synthesis. 'It is only a variation on the same theme when one hears of a renaissance of sciences, of the function of sociology and biology, the doing away with specialisation, or when visual artists fight for a pure painterly style, against Impressionism and for decoration. Everywhere we have, instead of the endless collecting of visual hints, a self-sufficient intellectual endeavour, which has already given a new ring to the despised words 'obstruction', 'system', and 'composition'.

Quoting directly from Matisse's *Notes d'un peintre*, which had been available in German translation since 1908, Raphael shows that the abandoning of Impressionism was a search for a new stability:[40]

> I prefer to take the risk of losing the individual stimulus by emphasising the character of the landscape. To make up for it I gain more stability. Behind the sequence of moments that constitute the ephemeral existence of essence and thing and lends them their mutable forms of experience, one can look for a truer, more essential character to which the artist will cleave, so as to give a more enduring interpretation of reality.[41]

'To the degree that in the art of creation, human activity has developed in its intellectual aspect especially, the artist has an increasing feeling for the activity of his own personality.'[42]

It is in the following paragraph one arrives at the distinction that captures for Raphael what is essential to the difference for artistic practise, and not just part of the antinomy of the generational; where he identified that in Impressionism, the losing oneself in nature, one sought to blur abstraction by depriving the unyielding evidence of the eyes of its effect in each and every sensuous area and thereby tried to come 'close to the impression of nature'. A 'passivity, characterised by an unheard of receptivity of all the senses, has a corresponding active *intellectuality* which – affirmative of the sensory receptivity – does not reproduce sensory impressions in order to re-awaken the feeling of the impression, but rather tries to form them for expressive purposes.'[43]

What characterises this expressive purpose is simplicity, clarity and pathos. Raphael objects to the deleterious consequences of the use of the term 'primitive', which has done so much damage in the understanding of this art. What is dismissed as primitive is in fact the complexity of Impressionism condensed and concentrated. Thus the 'primitive' is nothing to do with the child-like or naïf; it is rather a synthesis, a simplification, actually a struggle in overcoming, not a denial.

The second feature after simplicity is clarity, and Raphael notes that Gauguin was the first to claim this as a title of fame. 'Since then it has been a law of the artist that everything has to be spread out on the surface clearly, that the picture has to have as great a visibility as possible.' Thirdly, and least expected, was the return of 'pathos', a term despised in the Impressionist worldview, and yet 'it was into just this despised expression that the young artists poured their burgeoning joy in artistic activity, a joy before which they had occasionally trembled as if before a mendacious phantom. Pathos had once again become creative joy that affirms everything that is, because it shapes it. It is an anti-bourgeois feeling because it is a creative one.'

The young artists belong nevertheless to their time, and Raphael approvingly quotes the statement of Matisse: 'All artists bear the mark of their time but the greatest ones are those who have let themselves be stamped most deeply by it. Whether we like it or not, and much as we would like to emphasise that we are refugees in this age, it still produces solidarity between itself and us from which none of us can escape.'[44]

Raphael is of course careful to strike a balance in saying that no aesthetic formulation, however perspicuous, can set the value of an art at nought. Thus in his other main article of 1911 discussing the New Secession, "The New Painting. The New Secession", he is careful to show that he is not denigrating the masterpieces of Impressionism. Raphael had taken from Leopold Ziegler's article in *Logos* the relevant critique of the Impressionist worldview: 'We sense nature in its eternal changing as the analogy of one of the works of time (…) hence one is a visual artist precisely to the extent that one can, in place of the eternal state of affairs, put the enduring object which one creates artificially, since neither nature nor experience offers it to him.'[45] It is important for the development of his position to see how much Ziegler's article exposes, as it were, the 'category' error of naturalism. As Raphael notes, there can be the most various relationships between nature and creative power besides that of slavish clinging. The Impressionists want to represent the object in relation to air and light, and not derive their conception, as was done in previous times, from the individual object by means of linear abstraction. Raphael then asks pertinently: Why shouldn't there be other new forms beyond this possibility as well?'

For the artists of the New Secession, '*sensation* is now the element determining form, so that it is no longer closeness to nature but the expression of feeling that is the aim of their work.' However, by expression of feeling it is not intended to say that this means any sentiment which comes into one's mind. The artist seeks to now find a colour-composition out of the first things in the visible world of appearance that arouses feeling in him, so that nature leaps out again, not – Raphael adds – 'as a phenomenal value, an augmented and clarified observation, a piece of the psychology of nature accidentally caught in the picture frame, but as a self-contained picture of her essence and character, under the condition of the complete annihilation of the object's significance through the medium of the artist; a concentrated, abstracted expression.' Again it is Matisse who has the most exemplary word: 'It is not possible for me to slavishly copy nature; I am obliged to interpret her and to subordinate her to the spirit of the picture. When I have discovered all the relationships of my colour-tones, a living concord of colour must arise from this, a harmony analogous to that of a musical composition.'[46]

Raphael attempts a formula with regard to the question of artistic creation and the relation to nature: in Impressionism personal devotion and personal reproduction dominate; among the young stylists it is personal devotion and impersonal reproduction. A third source allows him the additional concept which is crucial for the new painters; it is from Maurice Denis:

> From the standpoint of subjectivity the thought 'nature seen through a temperament' is replaced by the theory of the equivalent, a symbol. We formulated the law that the feelings or spiritual states caused by a certain event provide the artist with signs or plastic equivalents which enable him to reproduce these feelings or spiritual states without having to counterfeit the actual drama; that our emotions must at every stage have a corresponding harmony in reality which enables us to translate them. Art is no longer a sensation which we absorb with our eyes (...) no, it is the creation of our intellect, to which nature has only given coincidental prompting. 'Instead of working with our eyes, we apprehend with the mysterious centre of thought', as Gauguin said (...) and art (...)

became the subjective transformation of nature. (...) In short, the expressive synthesis, the symbol of a sensation now has to be reproduced by a penetrating description and at the same time be a work of art pleasing to the eye.[47]

To this Raphael adds the comment: 'With these last words the aim of the new movement is elucidated: the closed composition.'

Raphael then goes to the implication of this argument on closed composition to understand what the new requirement for painting is, thereby making sense of his programmatic if esoteric formulation about the relation to the wall of his earlier responses, in which he saw Pechstein as excelling: Impressionist artists did not have an obligatory relationship between the picture format and representation, the surface could be indeterminate in its size. Content could also be taken at will from the stream of appearances. The artists who think by means of and for the wall, however, compose under the coercion of the picture surface, and thus an enlargement or reduction is impossible. 'For every surface-area one must conceive anew. Apart from the format, the surface itself compels. Everything of the object must stay in the surface. Spatial composition is eliminated. On this surface the colours are flat, evenly painted out and, insofar as they describe objects, nailed to the surface with a contour line. This line, occasionally black, more often a contrast in tone or colour, has become a painterly means and a powerfully expressive marking in its elasticity and richness of content. It does not create form, but rather circumscribes it, expresses sensation.

As Raphael argues in this article, the contrast between colour perceptions, and those used by the Impressionists, can be formulated in Fechner's law, the differences between stimuli are reduced in inverse proportion to their intensities.[48] Because one wants colour to express, Raphael continues, one dispenses with its minute division and optical mixing. The artist prefers to increase deliberately the materiality of the paint, the 'dark saturated colours of the spectrum', and paints them out in large masses. Impressionists had emphasised the qualities of the colours and tried to establish the laws of their relationships scientifically, but for Raphael the young artists found expressive possibilities in the scientific quantitative calculations of a sort that was most individual and capable of variation.

These young artists were often regarded as idiots by critics and people 'unable to regard works of art as the expression of a full, strong and energetically streaming power of artistic creation', because, Raphael argues, 'they fail to recognise the seriousness and strenuous, laborious efforts of the artists. One overlooks the immense breadth of this movement, which is long at home in literature and is about to conquer the theatre. This is not whim, but conviction, and the battle is fought under that banner.'[49]

There we have Raphael's joining the fray and the battle on the side of the new movement. In a few short weeks he will give it a name, for the first time in the German language, and will set out again what its principal features are, indeed features that would rapidly become distorted by later advocates of Expressionism, whose historical sense and critical acumen drove the movement into a tendentious relationship with the Gothic and made of it a particular German national style. Raphael's analysis then accepts the relativism of the pictorial subject, as announced by Denis, and even – one can add – the loss of an autonomous visual aspect to objects, as with Cézanne, this announced a principle of the flatness of the surface and the construction of an internally harmonious thing, which in Kandinsky's sense, whose *On the spiritual in art* was written at this time, is a picture. The picture could create its own reality, and colours assembled in a certain way were the symbolic form of expression for the painter. Raphael had visited Kandinsky in this year, and was effectively announcing and soliciting for a book manuscript which he was to publish and, on Kandinsky's report to Marc, described as a study on the psychology of artistic creation.[50]

In a detailed review of the drawings exhibition of the Secession, which he published under the title "White and Black", Raphael broaches again the problem of how work is exhibited. In this article there is some ambivalence still with respect to the strengths of the older and younger generation, and how they relate to each other. If drawings can lead directly into the workshop of the psyche of the artist by showing the most direct utterances, one who feels an intimate relationship would be 'frightened off by the impossible panes of glass or ugly differences in height.'

The transformation of Raphael's position is fairly complete. He is now a an active protagonist in the emergence of the generational revolt, has aligned himself with the elements which he identifies as anti-bourgeois, and has effectively drawn out the theoretical distinctions between Impressionism and the work of the younger generation into a wider notion of a movement which also includes literature and theatre. It is for the moment a speculation that the article in which he would name this movement derived its inspiration for the German neologism 'Expressionismus' – which would come to act as its broad term and placeholder – from the text of Denis. It is clear that Raphael had this in mind from the early summer of 1911, when he writes to Piper Verlag in Munich to propose a book, which would later result in the publication of *Von Monet zu Picasso*.[51]

Pechstein's break with the New Secession was the catalyst for the show which Raphael reviews and for his direct polemical engagement against Lovis Corinth. Raphael had set out his theoretical position around the concept of the creation of 'the picture', and had criticised the Impressionists not for their procedures, since Impressionism had freed painting from what he termed a 'cosy academicism'. In "Liebermann's Good Samaritan", he argues that in its deign the picture proceeds from the whole. 'Before the artist can begin to record his sensation, it must have been so long in the shaping and modelled in him that a completeness, a picture, has emerged from the fullness and multiplicity of natural impressions and visual images, that from now on determines every single form from within itself, from its life and existence.' Raphael makes a crucial argument here, to create 'something new, something that was not there before', asserting that 'one needs to have overcome both nature and oneself, to have formed out of the play of both a third element.' This result is of course the picture, 'the clear, visual, total conception.' It is a conception to which one must subordinate 'every natural form and every connection with personal experience in order to derive from it the justification, transformation or rejection of each and every motif.' It is for those reasons that Raphael thinks naturalism is incapable of picture-creation. Naturalism subordinates representation to natural forms and justifies itself by appealing to 'the natural truth of personal apprehension'. The totality already appears in the finished product, 'the solution that results from the summation of independently co-existing parts and details.'

Where, in Raphael's argument, the artist bases his pictorial creation on a total conception, he 'becomes a free creator from a certain moment in the creative process. As soon as he has condensed the sensation to a total conception, as soon as the principal masses, lines colours and lights have sorted themselves out in his intellect, he can work consciously and freely at giving these main bearers the strongest possible expression.' Within the play between nature and personality that leads to a third element, there is another play within the life of the artist:

> After he has formed the experience between the conscious and the unconscious, he will now be able as an adept to work out, so to speak, the clearest, most emphatic and yet simplest effect. If he knows what principle lines are called for he will be able to strengthen them with another curvature. The same applies to colour and light. The artist can strengthen here, weaken there, with no regard for, or consideration of nature or for fixed connections, just as it seems called for, only by the harmony and life of the whole. For he no longer derives his laws from nature, but from the picture. The picture, however, is something stable, a situation, so to speak – the contrary of all tendencies of movement and time of the Impressionists.

In a complex move, by analysing the failure of Liebermann with respect to picture creation, Raphael tries not only to irrevocably finish off the 'old' Secession, but to demonstrate where the actual painterly failure lies, whilst still keeping intact his respect for the work of Liebermann, whom he takes as really the strongest of the older generation of artists.

Liebermann's failure is not about subject matter – in this instance the parable of the Good Samaritan from the Gospel of Luke, a story that Raphael feels has such universal expressiveness that it can 'absorb the modern sensibility also'. It is not the subject matter that is at fault, but the Impressionist tendency to destroy 'the real life of things in favour of the varying moments of the atmosphere. (…) One must turn the spiritual into a still-life.' However, Liebermann has made progress towards the picture in for example his Brandenburg landscape, where one can see the 'resolute simplification and cutting down into large areas. One sees how the individual tree-trunks are positioned entirely in relation to the figures. But that doesn't stop the foreground, with its Italian flatness, from falling out of the picture or prevent the figure-groups from being two separate, unconnected parts, nor does it prevent the high total tone of the picture from being too brightly pitched for the subject matter.'[52] The specific observation that follows is very precise: the advancing figure from the right hand background is indeed picturesque, but in terms of its tonality it is counter-productive to the expression. All that remains is a certain piquancy in the purely artistic element.

Raphael thinks that with their links to the tradition of Corot, the French artists are far in advance of the German. However, Pechstein's gifts 'have given the clearest justification of his tendencies and personality, whatever shape his career might take.' The generation divide is shockingly clear. However, the antithesis is not just 'how quickly and how rightly one has accustomed oneself to the epithet "old"':

> (…) one does not become any younger when one prescribes oneself a dose of stale *so-called* Expressionists from Paris, a painter of kitsch like Manguin (…), an Othon Friesz (…), an adulteration of Cézanne (…) All that is left is de Vlaminck and the youthful works of Picasso; one does not become younger when one writes about a national German artistic youth and can show no more than a hopeless reality (…) Mister Corinth should not write that, should not write at all; he betrays that his mind has become academic, or that it always was, and invokes words in my memory which come from Apollinaire's satirical pen: 'L'ignorance et la frénésie, voilà bien les caractéristiques de l'Impressionisme.'[53]

Notably, this is the first reference in the published writing of Raphael to 'the youthful works of Picasso'. He will reprise his study of Picasso later in a section of *Von Monet zu Picasso*. The direct, full frontal attack on Corinth signals Raphael's last vestige of attachment to what the older generation wanted to hold onto. He has now fully joined the battle for the future of art in the imperial capital of Berlin. Corinth's article in the 13th number of *Pan* leads to a withering reply, and in the heat of the polemic Raphael himself becomes the *nomothete*, the name giver, who defines the movement, the medium and the message. One may speak of the 'invention of Expressionism' as a *fait accompli*.

NOTES

1. I would like to thank Professor Claude Schaefer in Paris for granting access to his biographical writings on Raphael and providing me with a complete photocopy of the "Biographie", which I cite from the manuscript. My paper and a complete reproduction of the manuscript along with a transcription will appear in the latter part of this year on the maxraphael.org website.

2. Max Raphael, *Von Monet zu Picasso* (Munich: Delphin Verlag, 1913]

3. Max Raphael, *The Demands of Art*, translated by Norbert Guterman (London: Routledge, 1968), with an introduction by Herbert Read. In a communication from Shirley Chesney I am informed that Herbert Read and Professor Robert Cohen were instrumental in bringing Raphael's work to the attention of the Bollingen Foundation. For more on this see Denise Modigliani's introduction to the French translation: *Questions d'art* (Paris: Klincksieck, 2008), pp.7–80. The edition of the *Lebenserinnerungen*, edited by Hans-Jürgen Heinrichs (Frankfurt-am-Main: Suhrkamp, 1989), remains the most complete collection of biographical information in print.

4. "Biographie", 1909–1910 (fol.2)

5. Fuller details can be found in Ron Manheim's "Max Raphael vor Max Raphael", in: Max Raphael, *Das schöpferische Auge*, ed. by Patrick Healy and Hans Jürgen Heinrichs, with an essay by Ron Mannheim (Gesellschaft für Kunst und Volksbildung), pp.132–161.

6. References and citations are from appearance of articles in German in *Das schöpferische Auge* (see note 5), and will be abbreviated as: *DSA*, page number. The reference here is from *DSA*, 17.

7. *DSA*, 18.

8. *DSA*, 18–19.

9. *DSA*, 20–21.

10. *DSA*, 21.

11. *DSA*, 22.

12. For this see my *Beauty and the Sublime* (Amsterdam: SUN, 2003), pp.83–105.

13. *DSA*, 23–24

14. *DSA*, 25.

15. *DSA*, 25–26.

16. *DSA*, 27.

17. *DSA*, 27–28.

18. *DSA*, 29.

19. *DSA*, 31.

20. *DSA*, 32.

21. *DSA*, 33.

22. *DSA*, 34.

23. *DSA*, 34.

24. *DSA*, 34. Further information see Magdalena Moeller, *Der Sunderbund* (Köln, 1984), and my article "Matisse and the Earliest Theory of German Expressionism", in *element*, 1 (1993), pp.29–36.

25. *DSA*, 34–35.

26. *DSA*, 35.

27. *DSA*, 37.

28. *DSA*, 75-81.

29. Donald E. Gordon, *Expressionism: Art and Idea* (Place: Yale University Press, 1987), p.113ff.

30. Nolde's autobiography is still in print; also see the recent *Emil Nolde, Mein Leben*, from Dumont.

31. Peter Gay, *Weimar Culture* (London: Penguin, 1968).

32. The article was published in the *Davoser Review*, 6, nr. 11 (15 August 1931).

33. German text can be found in Max Raphael, *Aufbruch in die Gegenwart*, ed. Hans-Jürgen Heinrichs (Suhrkamp, 1989), pp.14–20.

34. The meeting with Matisse is reported in an article he wrote for *Das Kunstblatt*, May 5, 1917, pp.145–154.

35. Peter Paret, *The Berlin Secession: Modernism and Its Enemies in Imperial Germany* (Harvard University Press, 1980).

36. *DSA*, 43–44.

37. *DSA*, 44.

38. *DSA*, 44.

39. *DSA*, 42.

40. *DSA*, 61.

41. See note 24 above.

42. *DSA*, 58.

43. *DSA*, 59.

44. *DSA*, 61.

45. *DSA*, 62.

46. *DSA*, 63–64.

47. *DSA*, 64.

48. Raymond E. Fancher, *Pioneers of Psychology* (New York, Norton, 1979), pp.132–144.

49. *DSA*, 67.

50. See note 4 above.

51. For this see the essay by Ron Manheim, note 5 above.

52. *DSA*, 73.

53. *DSA*, 73–74.

CRITICAL WRITINGS
1910-1913

THE AMERICAN EXHIBITION

I quote Wilde, the last great sun-worshipper:

'The sun drives thought back even further, and it must seek refuge in the shade. Thought dwelt in Egypt once – but then that land was conquered by the sun. It lived a long time in Greece, but it too fell to the sun, as did Italy and then France. Nowadays one meets thought always as a refugee, exiled all the way to Norway and Russia where the sun never comes. The sun is jealous of art.'[1]

One doesn't have to be a lyrically enthusiastic sun-worshipper, leaning on the walls of S. Apollinare in Classe Fuori on the highway from Pinienhain to Ravenna,[2] to revere the setting sun. It is not necessarily an unconscious after-effect of the sun-cult when fiery sunset clouds remind us of the aureoles of primitive pictures of Jesus; even the sober academic brain can point out connections between the course of the sun and the path taken by culture.

If we use a globe to put our historical knowledge in order, we begin right in the East, in China, from where our thoughts move on to India and Persia, and from there to Egypt on the one hand and to Greece (by way of Asia Minor), Italy and France on the other. Here the ocean checks the flight of our thoughts, a new world begins on the other side, the western hemisphere: America, the west coast of which is, like our starting-point, washed by the Pacific Ocean. Picking up Japan, we complete our circle, with its end placed right beside its beginning. To be sure, I have used an analogy to anticipate my conclusion.

So we traverse that world history which we know from east to west, following the course of the sun, if one can be forgiven the solecism; our attention is held by the area between the Northern Tropic and the Arctic Circle or, more exactly limited, between the thirtieth and fiftieth parallels. If we regard this area as that of the lands of culture, those bordering it as outsiders with tasks appropriate to them *vis-à-vis* the sun, then we can ascribe the rigid, cold, cerebral and doubt-filled aspects of cultural development to the north, and those instinct with feeling and belief to the south.

I denoted the circle as the symbol to represent all of history, without giving it a *function* among the individual periods which make up the whole. The rising line of the optimist, the falling one of the pessimist does not do it either; it is the spiral, almost closing in a circle, winding inwards in almost parallel curves and then outwards again in a similar movement from an inmost point – it is this line which symbolises the event. Better still, let us think of the outward-developing line as being marked with a red core which gets gradually wider and thus shows the burgeoning content of the next period.

It would be an idle question to try to establish the number of spirals there have been so far. All we can say is that they are completely similar as far as content is concerned, provided we abstract this content sufficiently. In the course of events it is forms, not contents that change. Form is the new; and in every single period a form is perfected, becomes the model, and it does so mostly at the expense of the others.

Today the knowledge of history is such that I have no need to emphasise either that periods are not separated by a chasm but rather flow into one another, or that each period has its corresponding form of art, determined by that form on which the age has stamped its special character. I think of Christendom and would like to bring to mind the grave. In its beginning, the course of historical development comes from what is determined by purpose only: a stone chest, a lid. It would be well worth analysing the aesthetic pleasure undoubtedly provided by this most primitive of shapes. Next we see relief on the sides, clumsy, crude but belonging there more than unexpected, far-fetched ones. The purpose is less and less to be seen, the great wall-tombs of Lombardy spring to mind; it becomes a mere pretext and rarely do we find mutually determined purpose and form in the highest works of art. Thus purpose stands at the beginning of artistic form, the principle of art for art's sake at the end.

And now we come to the period of Christianity. We know that the Nazarene's great thought had been prepared beforehand in the sunset of Greece, so that we can view it as the most successful type of all earlier attempts. He brought the democratisation of religion, the faith of the tax-collector. It was his tragedy that the popes established their aristocratic hierarchy in complete opposition to his teachings. His true disciples were always the enemies of the papacy, they who announced to one and all that they had the right to commune with their god and so on: Francis of Assisi, Luther.

The age of Christianity, that is to say, the battle to democratise the faith, ended with the French Revolution. The *ancien régime* offers us the picture of the fall of an aristocratic society; one goes right to the scaffold with a proud laugh. Life was a game in which one was prepared for everything and one was up to any challenge, above all to meet death with a smile and a quip. Thus Christianity and its aristocracy died a proud dance of death on the shores of the ocean, the great sea, on the holiest soil of Christian culture. Rousseau's false sentimentality was the only false note in this masque of death. The new cult of reason celebrated its resurrection, a bizarre and laughable picture. Any Christian and pious impulse that the nineteenth century received from the Romantics was not an organic development, but a resuscitation of the dead. Everywhere art lies under the false influence of science or gives off the delicate rotting smell of our sublimest Impressionists and lyricists. In its lonely hiding-place behind the confusion of pictures and books, made for *those* very few who have developed every sense to its finest filament, we find art for art's sake: purposeless art, useless art, the only art of our time. This time the aristocracy is still there, decaying in every area: Monet, Stefan George, Nietzsche, defending itself against the new form of democratisation, that of economic life and all art deriving from it.

I have already named one factor in this new germinal period: reasonable reason. The others go back into the time of Christianity: the extension of the money economy and the discovery of America. America has become the country in which the democratisation of economic life has shown itself in the purest forms in all areas: in the satisfaction of daily wants, in organisations and so on. It is *actually* clear that also a new art will emerge, diverging from the European and corresponding to these new forms. Like every previous art form, it will develop from those needs and purposes which belong to this period and this people only. The historian knows from the history of Venice, for example, that the process of forming an art out of new conditions does not happen in decades, or even in a few centuries. Apart from that, every ethnopsychologist emphasises – and is it really with complete justification – the pronounced artistic inability of the American people. Moreover, we know that the first new forms – autochthonous and intransportable, as it were – have to be sought in their homeland, where one will surely find them. One can only go to the 'so-called' American Exhibition with great scepticism. What did Mr Reisinger show us in the Academy? To say it straight away: no art based on American soil, no art growing from conditions there, from national idiosyncrasy. Instead a variety of French art, pictures created from European influences, which only demonstrate national character in the appreciation and exploitation of impressions, that is to say, in the choice of models and in their transformation. Here we see the upper limits of *their* artistic powers, which are too weak for autonomous, primary creation.

The contents are the same as in Europe: the portrait, the interior, and the landscape. This last is the mother of our modern painting, and here the French of the older and newer schools have produced the best. In spite of all confusion of ideas I cannot define the essence of French Impressionism at this point. It has affected the American artist as it has those of other nations. Unable technically to represent the finer moods, they escaped by closely following the Barbizon masters, then Monet and the Impressionists. But they achieved neither the high seriousness of the former nor the subtle delicacy of the latter. The landscapes have an unpleasant sweetness in the colour which suggests a truly sentimental yet glancing relationship to nature. For none of the landscapes displays a penetration of nature equal to that of the French, and just here where the ultimate problems of Impressionism are propounded, in the representation of quivering foliage, for example, a vivifying breath is missing which may lead back to a discrepancy between technical ability and artistic need. One feels a want, even more when the naturally gigantic, the savagely imposing is to be represented; then the impressions are almost unpleasant.

The Americans, always with the exception of Whistler, are nowhere personalities or artistic types more creative than the run of the mill French artist. Must we then conclude that the mixed people of America is artistically incapable? I am much more inclined to see a definite strength of artistic sensibility in this firm rejection of the western European art of decadence, an artistic sensibility directed completely at other things, at the creation of new works, to Europeans almost alien. When we are analysing our culture we must in any case distinguish between that which belongs to the death-bed of the Christian era, and bears the most refined marks of art for art's sake, and that which one must call Americanism, *but not in a* bad sense, that is all those forms which develop in a new way from new requirements.

As Johannes V. Jensen[3] says in his collection of essays *Die Neue Welt*:[4] 'American houses are built in a truly heathen style. By this I mean when they built them they had their use in mind, their benefits, before they ever thought of architecture. One will see later that this style is beautiful. For beauty follows truth, as it does strength.'

Originally published as: Max Raphael-Schönlanke, "Die Amerikanische Ausstellung", in: *März*, IV, 12 (Mid-June, 1910), pp.497–500.

NOTES

1. Wilde in a letter to André Gide, written in French.

2. Sant'Apollinare in Classe, Ravenna (Italy): Byzantine basilica, 1st half of the 6th century.

3. Johannes Vilhelm Jensen: Farsø, 1873 – Copenhagen, 1950. Danish author.

4. Johannes Vilhelm Jensen, "Die Maschinen", in: *Die Neue Welt: Essays* (Berlin: Fischer, 1908), p.46.

BERLIN EXHIBITIONS

Anyone who has ever crossed the borders of naive experience within which one feels oneself at one with nature and the supernatural, anyone who has come consciously to experience his surroundings and his own self and has felt the chasm that has now opened between him and the objects, will be shocked by the chaotic confusion of phenomena and strive to overcome it. Every human effort, even in the purely material area, can be thus interpreted without sophistry. One can define art as the shaping of this chaotic play through art's specific means. One will have grasped the nerve of a work of art when one can say how the artist approached nature, the sequence of images, how it mirrors itself in his imagination, how he conceives it and forms it with his means. Here Zola found his explanation of the work of art, the most embracing of our time: '*un oeuvre d'art est un coin de la nature vu à travers un temperament.*'[1] Of the two elements nature is the enduring, constant one, but not for everyone alike. For the temperament shows itself in the choice of the 'coin de la nature'. This is variable and hence the determining factor.

It follows from this that the number of art works can be just as limitless as the number of individuals. With this breadth of explanation one seems to have posited a nihilistic plethora of possibilities. One can see how fine these differentiations can be when one takes temperaments like Trübner[2] and Liebermann[3] for comparison. Although they share a virile energy, one begins to detect the nuances in their techniques; this is the handwriting of character. Trübner places his dots cleanly side by side. When one is close up to the canvas one can enjoy the pleasure of the artist in the purity of beautiful matter and its beautiful purposeful positioning. The surface is an ornamental striped pattern. When one stands back, one gradually senses a virile energy behind these artistic enjoyments, one which produces the play of light and shadow, the growth through light and air of an organism in its beauty, the essence of the soil, the rooting of the tree. His work gives us the whole force, the brutality even of the real phenomena. One comes to the picture again. We find the painter's love in the powerful tones of colour which reach the strength of those in nature. One loves this intoxication through decorative colour, the beauty of the tones, the means having no purpose but themselves.

Not so Liebermann. Close up his canvas is like a messy palette. His stroke is thin, jagged and nervous. When one steps back, his surfaces acquire first form and then spatial relationships to each other. Then space begins to sing and sound unexpected never heard melodies, and mystified one asks: How? One is astonished at the colourlessness, but also at the wealth and exactness of gradation, every tone of which characterises. Every false gradation is like an ungerminated seed. The entire colour is mere means, insignificant in itself, necessary for the formation of the whole.

Behind these characteristic differences lie things in common, mutually connecting, peculiar to this time. One could, by abstracting sufficiently, read the handwriting of today's characters from the technique. The next question concerns the fundamental feelings in common which determine the creation and are mirrored in these works. It is the attitude of delicate sensibility, of passive relativity, of knowledge of oneself.

This delicate sensibility allows the artist to react to external impressions with undreamt of sharpness. One sees new nuances in the play of light, the subtlest gradations of colour; one senses new stimuli in the co-existence of what is in space and side by side, before and behind; one experiences the impalpable movements, the inaudible tones. One forgets the solitary. One experiences the mood, the air of a man or of a landscape. The eye sees all sense impressions, it hears the wind and smells the perfume, it feels the nerves.

The feeling of relativity deprives man today of the Christian viewpoint as the centre of existence, as the purpose of everything. He feels himself in accordance with the perceptions of science, to be of no more than equal value to the other organisms of nature; he has a feeling of himself only in relation to these conditions and in connection with them, and no longer exists just for himself. This restricts his activeness compared to that of earlier generations, who believed that they owned the world when they conquered it.

But not completely. The need for superiority has produced a fine growth. Man knows the objects. So does the animal, but man knows his knowledge. This gives him superiority. The artist, who next to the philosopher does the most self-reflection, can penetrate to a certain limit only, if creation is not to be inhibited. And this limit seems a very forward position now. These pictures give me the impression that the artist feels the whole weight of his subjective self and at the same time the unsureness of his superiority, which he himself threatens.

One has found the technical means to express this new spiritual attitude. Appropriate to the delicacy of sensibility we see a profound penetration of nature, a discovery of her charms, which are so new and various that one has not recognised them in their full depth in Cézanne, for example. The effect of relativity is to arrange the objects in a living sensuous atmosphere, to take from them their individual charms, and thus neutralise them so that they become passive, accepting, just like the creating subject. Arising from this unsure and forced knowledge is a grotesque element that I sense just as much in the piety and reverence of Monet as I do in the sharpness and abstraction of Liebermann.

There is a common thread too in the individual's development, in which first nature – the phenomenon – is emphasised, and later temperament. In this return to observation I see the fundamental value of this school, which has developed a general idea of style from the naturalistic representation of phenomena. After having transformed a piece of nature to the point of monumentality, one attempts to work creatively on this massive material. One conspicuous feature of our exhibition is the way they have occupied themselves with history painting. Liebermann brought his *Samson and Delilah*[4] here in 1903. It can be claimed for this picture that it has been created exclusively from the means so hard won from our contemporary style. But it is not so with the younger generation. This time Slevogt[5] brings his great canvas *The Hörselberg*,[6] Beckmann a working of the *Dispensation of the Holy Ghost*. The drawbacks of the material have been avoided, as far as that is possible for our time. For they have become familiar to us through Wagner and confirmed through our own experience; they have not however, come to mean more than the personal formation of a few congenial spirits. Slevogt has completely fallen victim to the greater dangers of picturesque composition. The main group and nothing else is rendered as phenomenon, the rest is academic pasteboard. Beckmann is more fortunate, his warring colours give something of the visionary nature of his subject. But if one wants a deeper concentration and more breadth of soul, one would first have to get rid of the unbridled formlessness of the composition and the sentimental banality of gesture.

One would be using the wrong yardstick if one compared these efforts with Puvis de Chavannes' cartoons[7], which are to be seen in the great exhibition. Only the towering personality and genius of the master could have worked up the Greek elements to such poetry and monumentality, to such an idiosyncratic personal expression of character. Perhaps this is the fulfilment. But we can be certain that we have a long way to go and can only reach our goal with patient creative work. Then the Hotspurs of today will have become the acknowledged masters. For behind these works one feels that the struggle to push back the boundaries of the age will be successful. By obeying that which one may call the 'must' of our time with as much energy as patience, the artists overcome their sense of creative limitation by the confident sense of building. They all have the character trait of yielding themselves and having confidence in becoming and in the development of events, the content of which they seek and hold up as a banner, like the pathfinders and leaders that they are. Their will transforms nature, the objects are their gods.

And what of this personality and its will? This ego that has no trust in fate? This individual who is neither willing nor able to lose himself in nature, who must rather dominate it? This is what the Romantics ask. Here, too, these opponents of the imperative of the day seem to produce as many works of art as there are individuals. They, however, derive their rules from themselves and not from the objects. But an individual can never create a style for an age. This can only be produced by a joint effort of the spirit in the contemporary imperative. They thus have the need to borrow eclectically and to work these borrowings into a personal means of expression or else to a rational scheme together. This is how Hofmann[8] and Hodler got to their ornamental stylisation. This explains their weakness: that they have to force the world into a compositional scheme, one which thanks to their great personalities is so broad that it masters the most extremely opposed phenomena and yet is coercive and one-sided. Their strength and power lies in the sureness and means of expression, which enables them to present the subject matter in a clearly articulated formal language. These people with their 'I must attain to the art of beauty', and anyone who has had the good fortune to see the Hofmann frescoes in the Weimar Theatre will be thankful to them. He has not always succeeded in so drenching his vehicle with his own lyrical Hellenic character. Here we see music, life, no longer just colours emphatic of feeling, stylised form and the rhythms of line. But if these means become an end in themselves, they atrophy into the decorative. And this is the second object of our young artists, the wish to form the laws of the spatial not out of the object, not out of themselves, but out of the wall and its mood. A decoration must be formed from the play of closed colour surfaces and lines. Here, perhaps, we find a difference in principle that has led to the founding of the New Secession. Pechstein[9] is the strongest temperament; we must wait to see what he brings us.

Originally published as: M.R. Schönlank, "Berliner Ausstellungen", in: *März*, IV, 15 (August 2, 1910), pp.234–237.

NOTES

1. 'A work of art is a corner of nature viewed through a temperament.' Emile Zola, *Mes haines* (originally published 1866).

2. Heinrich Wilhelm Trübner: Heidelberg, 1851 – Karlsruhe, 1917. Painter. Member of the Berlin Secession from 1901.

3. Max Liebermann: Berlin, 1847 – Berlin, 1935. Painter, graphic artist, illustrator. Founding member and leader of the Berlin Secession, 1899–1911.

4. Max Liebermann. *Samson and Delilah*. 1902. Oil on canvas. 150 x 212 cm. Städelsches Kunstinstitut, Frankfurt am Main.

5. Max Slevogt: Landshut, 1868 – Leinsweiler, 1932. Painter, graphic artist.

6. Max Slevogt. *Der Hörselberg*. 1910. Oil on canvas. Bayerische Staatsgemäldesammlung, Munich.

7. Pierre Puvis de Chavannes: Lyon, 1824 – Paris, 1898. Symbolist painter, known for large-scale works in mural or fresco.

8. Ludwig von Hofmann: Darmstadt, 1861 – Pillnitz, 1945. Painter, graphic artist, book illustrator.

9. Max Pechstein: Zwickau, 1881 – Berlin, 1955. Painter, graphic artist. Founding member of the New Secession; joined Die Brücke in 1906.

A BOOK ON MANET

Cassirer has published a document the contents and get up of which add up to make a valuable contribution to the understanding of the Impressionists; it is *Edouard Manet: Sein Leben und seine Kunst*, by Théodore Duret.[1]

Of the subtitle's two aims, the author has fulfilled the first one perfectly. Duret gives us a developing artist's life in the round, in a style which combines the clarity of the empathising connoisseur, the inner joy of the fellow conqueror and the delicate irony of the superior intellect. He shows us the social milieu of the reserved and educated bourgeoisie into which Manet was born, and how this complete gentleman, this lover of brilliant salons, who seems to have grown into a Parisian boulevardeer, has retained this distinguished character throughout his life. This tradition gives him stability, but it does not tie him down. He fights against it whenever he wants to assert himself: against his parents, against the academic trumpery of his teachers, against juries and critics, against the public with its habit and its stupidity. He recognises his own worth with a great instinctive certainty and his vanity and ambition demand full recognition and brilliant triumphs. By showing us all phases of resistance, the mockery, scorn and derision which was heaped upon him, Duret provides us with a valuable contribution to the psychology of the public which for decades fought against accepting this nature-mirroring art.

Duret shows us this art in all its many-sidedness and in the uninterrupted progress of its development. He sets us in front of the easel and we experience the creation of his portrait, a process which is discussed in detail. The individual works are always analysed with fine understanding; the canvas becomes a living experience for us. Here the author's intentions have been given the best possible support by the publisher. The really carefully chosen photographs have been reproduced sharply and clearly. Two original etchings and the colour woodcut are also valuable; together with some well-reproduced drawings, they convey to us the immediate feeling of Manet's hand and the shiver of creation. With such an outstanding book one is not afraid to mention a fault: we miss an analysis of Manet's individual manner, a precise exposition of his style.

Originally published as: M.R. Schönlank, "Ein Manetbuch", in: *März*, IV, 18 (August 2, 1910), pp.494–495.

NOTES

1. Théodore Duret, *Histoire d'Éduard Manet et de son oeuvre* (Paris: Floury, 1902). Translated into German in 1903.

THE SONDERBUND IN DÜSSELDORF

For the wanderer who has seen many cities it is always a special experience to arrive in Düsseldorf and to be captured and enveloped by this city's atmosphere before one has even gone a few steps. One picks it up even in the Königsallee. To one's left the noble calm of a Residence City of medium rank, to one's right the discreetly smiling to and fro of a flourishing commercial city, which is home also to a rich industrial hinterland. With its purchasing power this gives the art of the region a clearly marked momentum, an impetus to the newer and the newest in tune with this society. All this has provided the Sonderbund with a suitable soil for this year's exhibition, in which the latest products of modern French painting are set up for comparison with those of Impressionism, an undertaking of an extent hitherto unknown in Germany. This sharp confrontation between two movements in art is a stimulus to a clarification and exposition of principles.

Impressionism is a personal attitude to the cosmos, one which creates by following nature, and this by the emphasis placed on the moving elements of light and air, by a character of deeply penetrating feeling and sensitivity. Impressionism, thus restricted in the type of artist and constrained in its choice of object, has been able to create a style; its narrow compass of the landscape has given it a general subject area, something which all good and fruitful artistic ages have done for themselves. In the Middle Ages the Church and its legends provided this material, and it was of the nature of the artist to be able to, by means of his personality, provide and invest these legends with spiritual content and to express this personal resuscitation of the dead with the power of his formative imagination. Today one must also be both, and the good Impressionist is: a personality and someone of ability.

The impression can be a double one. Firstly, a sensation of the momentary in which only the life of the instant is to be found. In this case, one shows one's personality through the number of moments perceived and expressed – whether one is able to convert just air or light alone into painterly terms or whether one can do this with the merest breeze, specific smell and finesse of movement etc. Then we have a sensation of the momentary that is a variation on the general, an expression of the instant that is nevertheless the whole soul of the landscape. One could speak of the impression of the inward. Here the personality will reveal itself to the degree in which its empathy has raised the invisible heart of the landscape to life in each of its momentary transformations. In the first case, Impressionism is more an international, and in the second case more a national mode of expression.

Whereas the Dutch have, thanks to their national instinct, remained fully national and the French have moved in both directions because of the power of their artistic gifts, the Germans have been completely international, although the not very mobile character of their vision would demand a completely national approach. But on the other hand they have been forced into this internationality of motif because the German landscape is generally too hard in its atmosphere, too immovable and, where it is mobile, too hidden, too difficult to catch. This unfortunate contingency has had the result that, all in all the Impressionist movement has foundered in Germany. One can see the truth of this for oneself in Düsseldorf.

Bretz,[1] who displays something of the idiosyncrasy of the Lower Rhine, something of the melancholy of the plain and of its loneliness, the loneliness with which a white house stands out against a green tree and blue shadows fall on the whitewash, and in the curve of the region's hills – no, Bretz is not an Impressionist. His emphasis is nearly always on the enduring, and thus he works more with line. Alterations caused by cosmic movements are to him more stimulus to mood than phenomena to be studied with the eye. Clarenbach,[2] the self-proclaimed pure Impressionist, has to yield a whole nuance of Impressionist ground when he tries to produce the character of the Lower Rhine. The sureness in the choice of a characteristic motif which would demonstrate a strong rational character is in him far more dubious even than in Bretz.

One could add a few more names without changing the verdict. All these artists lack a strong personality. With an excess of technical ability, they still have too little to say. They demand too little of themselves, they are too content with themselves. For they either lack unashamed honesty or sufficient diligence.

Not so Liebermann, whom the Düsseldorf artists have chosen as master, and with good reason they have made him their only honorary member. He is a very definite character, an industrious artist and a vigorous critic of his own work. If one sees him confront nature, follows him there, one can easily assign him his place among the Impressionists. What characterises him is his feeling for space, for monumental line, which has a slightly grotesque effect, and for bodily movement. The painterly means which produce this are more colourist than tonal. He conquers colour hue by hue, but in such a way that each is judged against a fine shade of grey that he finds at the seashore at certain times, at certain levels of the tide. He reaches his limits when he composes history. This year's *Samson and Delilah*[3] is also a failure.

Of the French Impressionist school Vuillard[4] is represented; he produces his sensitive impression of total mood by areas of thin colour on a ground which also becomes part of the effect. Signac is there too, with three pictures in which he brings the splitting-up of colour to its highest pitch. He places his dots of blue, red, green and yellow side by side like tesserae so that, through their contrasting play of mood, he can reproduce the air and light of nature with increased distinctness. One has come from nature and finally arrives through technical means at decoration. For how can these pictures fail to remind us of Ravenna? The difference that here a space is created whereas the mosaics are merely surfaces, is perhaps less decisive than the loose spread-out-ness of the colours. The mosaic's linear contour is absent; everything must be synthesised by the viewer. But once one goes back a certain desired distance, nature recaptures its objective forms, the pattern of dots can no longer defy synthesis.

The new painting has been consciously, decoratively flat from the outset; a decoration achieved through the insights into colour attained by the Impressionists. By this I mean that nature has lost every objective value and that the artist's imagination, working as it does with colours, has now won for itself a limitless, unbridled freedom.

In his foreword to the catalogue, Dr. Niemeyer has the following to say about the emergence of this painting: 'Impressionism was superseded (?!)[5] by the style of Cézanne, the logical extension of Manet's optical syntheses which, after the atmospherical absolutism of landscape art, once again taught one to understand painting as the pure creation of colour. His art (…) presented the new generation with the problem of conglomerating the inconceivable sum of the optical faces of nature into colour surfaces which are clear and simple and suffused with the breath of the most delicate contrasts, of comprehending the functional unity of bodily appearance, air and space as a closed system of colour values. His own creations (…) succeeded with their mysteriously floating colours in revealing that which is optical and intellectual throughout the material world, the inward immateriality of everything material. By giving the strange, fantastical look of the simple and great to the fragmentary multiplicity of reality they imprisoned the unfathomable dreaminess of things in their colourful mirror image. In its massively sculptural structure and its simplification of form, Cézanne's painting signifies the reaction of the deepest Roman feelings against the clear, more northerly manner of Impressionism, with its subtle analysis of optical phenomena. If the latter style reflected the multiplicity and movement of all nature with its manifold splitting up of colour and its rapid momentary application of paint, then Cézanne's picture responds to the impression of nature with the unity of floating colours. After Cézanne, Matisse has most recently gained influence on artistic youth by enacting the linear essence from Cézanne's sculptural constructions.' And with the zeal of the theoretician he takes up arms for the new doctrine.[6]

His pictures too have the effect of classical examples of the type. The picture is no longer an abundance of seemingly arbitrarily positioned points or specks of colour, but divided up into two or three large colour surfaces. The artistic power is expressed in the rhythm in which areas reciprocate one another and in which bodies are placed on these surfaces; then in the balancing of colours, which must have a particular ring, since they have to be seen in large areas. One wants to have form, but not that of nature. One wants rather the subjectively decorative, hence the line is neither formation, formative, nor an expression of form, but a decorative outline or inline which betrays the artist's character by its curves.

That the products which originate from this basis differ greatly from one another is a result of the subjective freedom which was already mentioned. We can see how much more can be got out of this by comparing the pictures of Kandinsky (Munich) with the dry sobriety of Matisse. Kandinsky's works seek the personal expression of a personal mood in a coloured composition. So he calls out full speed ahead with his shades of green, blue, red and ochre. And if the public think that only one who is mentally ill could produce and understand such an objectless splatter (question: 'what does this represent?'), so be it. But the pictures remind one of marvellous Nordic wall hangings, one must surely enjoy that.

One is always looking for chances to make comparisons with nature; one's meagre training is for this. Here one's model has completely disappeared. The artist no longer receives his laws from the object; the mirror of his imagination is everything. Science and imitation making have vanished again in favour of making anew.

One would certainly wish that these new pictures would be hung in a new way also, i.e. appropriate to their inner demand. They belong not in a frame on the wall, but without a frame in the wall.

Originally published as: M.R. Schönlank, "Der Sonderbund in Düsseldorf", in: *Nord und Süd*, XXXV, vol. 135, H.2 (2nd October issue, 1910), pp.154–157.

NOTES

1. Julius Bretz: Wiesbaden, 1870 – Bad Honnef, 1953. Painter, lithographer. Founding member of the Sonderbund, 1909.

2. Max Clarenbach: Neuss, 1880 – Wittlaer, 1952. Painter. Founding member of the Sonderbund, 1909.

3. Max Liebermann. *Samson and Delilah*. 1902. Oil on canvas. 150 x 212 cm. Städelsches Kunstinstitut, Frankfurt am Main.

4. Edouard Vuillard: Cuiseaux, 1868 – La Baule, 1940. French painter, graphic artist. Member of the post-Impressionist group Les Nabis.

5. Raphael's insertion.

6. Wilhelm Niemeyer, "Vorrede", in: *Ausstellung des Sonderbundes westdeutscher Kunstfreunde und Künstler. Düsseldorf 1910*, exhibition catalogue (Düsseldorf, 1910), pp.7–16.

BERLIN, WORLD CITY

History means migration. This narrow definition by a Berlin philologist can easily be proved by examples. There are two kinds of migration, one pressing forwards, the other flooding back. The first is directed from East to West. Barbarians force their way into a highly-cultivated country and create a new culture on its soil with their unused energy. The motives are admittedly of an economic nature. The second kind goes from West to East. At a certain precisely determined point in their history, civilised people overrun the home of a high but dead culture. The motives are almost always camouflaged with an ideal. Examples of this are the Dorian migrations and Alexander's campaign, the great migrations and the crusades. In our own age we have seen the emigration to America. Apart from these long-distance treks, under certain conditions all peoples have known the so-called flight from the land, i.e. the migration of the rural population to the city. Too few people in the country, too little room, too much crush in the city. This movement has no great breadth or extent; it is played out on a narrower stage, its motives are once again economic, and it is perhaps characteristic that to think of Berlin is to think of a migration from East to West.

This centre of humanity, growing in the way I have just described, seems at first sight to be ahead of other cities in extent and size. Its needs seem to be the same as that of other big cities, as are the means of satisfying them. But the problem remains whether, if the quantity increases beyond a certain point, the quality must also change. Naturally the business of administration in a city like Berlin will at first have a sharper, more charged efficiency than that of other cities. But are a department store in Düsseldorf and the biggest department store in the world not also completely different things qualitatively? One will be at first completely astonished by the increase in numbers and dimensions, especially since the outward forms required by new qualities develop only gradually and are harder to apprehend. One first learns to recognise and love the novelties of a great metropolis in what is visible, palpable, in the changes in the streetscape.

I do not wish to speak in general of the world city and its new forms, but only of Berlin, the most hated of them. Let me bring you to Krögel, a narrow lane, most painterly in its pinched darkness. Crowing cocks, quacking ducks, cobbler and blacksmith, hammering, barefoot, dirty children, dark and rickety wooden steps. Painterly, altogether ruinous. The Spree flows by the end of the lane, a colourful crowd bustles on deck of the slow-moving, groaning steamers, the famous apple barges of Berlin, the first form of trade and transport. How slowly and asthmatically they splutter their way compared to the underground, for which a neighbouring group of buildings is about to be pulled down. Seven hundred years of history lives between apple barge and the underground. But when one thinks about it, almost nowhere does one find the necessity for development. On the long road from fishing village to world metropolis that is how it was, but – apart from the last forty years – it could also have been completely different. Whenever I have come to know the heart of a city I have stood in awe before its inevitability. Berlin however, and it was never pious, makes one atheistic. Nothing is inevitable, one can imagine everything differently, except the underground. The stuff of existence is here like sand, that most minute substance. Fleeting, unenduring, just matter, minute matter. It needs to endure its physical and spiritual forms. It has no pattern and is thus ripe for anything; that is Berlin. But one searches the history of the city in vain for the great structuring genius who inspired this inferior matter with life and mind. Here, as in an anthill, it was the mass which created. Berlin is sand, brought together and formed and made to turn by millions of industrious, busily productive hands. Where do we find a structure as big, as necessary, as characteristic as this emergent Berlin?

This is the main objection to Berlin: that is it is ugly and characterless. Whether beautiful or ugly, we'll leave to the self-conscious aesthetes to decide. Even the young Goethe saw art as being beyond the beautiful and the ugly (see the so little read, so valuable Erwin von Steinbach[1]). This city as form and shaper of the human is, one says, without character. I concede that Berlin's atmosphere has a levelling effect. But suppose this was strength of character, a necessity. Our exponents of culture do not have to find soil in Berlin which is suitable for their culture, they have instead to be assimilated in it, democratised, because Berlin is home to a culture different to theirs. But in spite of the short span of forty years Berlin is already producing adequate characters, and soon one will speak of the Berliner as one does of the

Parisian, the inhabitant of Munich etc., and not as one did before in the negative sense of a grumbler and know all. In his book *Berlin*, Scheffler[2] characterises the Berliner with the words: He is 'doomed: *always to becoming and never to be.*'[3] Anyone who is a better psychologist than our novelist will have met a type that cannot be characterised otherwise. He is the enemy of all harmony, his life is an eternal to and fro; he is the modern Ahasver, perpetually wandering and restless. I will use just one very typical utterance to characterise him: A gentleman, puzzled by activity, complains to his friend about the unbearable stillness of the Nikolassee villas. His friend reacts by asking him where he would rather have one built. 'On Spittelmarkt', is the reply.

We have no right to form value judgements. Subsequent developments will not ask if we liked these people or not. And it characterises Berlin's strength that it has been able to produce a type in forty years. Those days after the war,[4] it lay there like a man who has just awoken, thirsty for deeds. Now it is a giant, albeit one whose first groggy movements may have occasioned follies, as the monstrous façades of the founding years prove. But berlin is sand and energy. In a few decades it will present a different picture. One will knock down and rebuild, and Berlin too will be a beautiful city. We now have every reason for a solemn joy.

The phenomenon of Berlin has become a problem to be addressed by the intelligentsia. The city's disciples bravely follow with restless energy; its enemies see it grow and spread its tentacles towards the old culture, they wave in front of every shop door, they want to see what they can get in exchange for the new. Hence all books written about Berlin are subjective and apologetic. Karl Scheffler was able to subtitle his book (published by Erich Reiss, Berlin – Westend, 1910) 'an exposition'. He tries to conceptualise *his* emotional impressions by analysing the history of the city. He finds valuable concepts, such as the colonial city. He makes it the basis of his analysis, which leads us through a conglomerate become artificial to the point where this affected creation finds its own culture, which is quickly rent to pieces however at the beginning of the last century. Then the metropolis develops, really at last beginning in 1870. Scheffler shows its varying destiny and goes on to close with a few worthwhile chapters such as "Utopia" and "Berlin's mission".

One can say nothing against books written from a personal angle, when the author's character is so upright, simple and interesting as Scheffler's, but he has written only *a* book about Berlin, not *the* book. That would require a method more allied to observation than his, more artistic than scientific. *The* book about Berlin would have to be written in short analytic impressions. A feeling of the street, the human, insofar as he is typical, should be conveyed in words that can bring the picture to immediate life. This says that only an artist and connoisseur of Berlin can write this book. To make myself clear, I will say that it may not be written like Huret's[5] book *Berlin*[6] (which appeared with Albert Langen in Munich). This book has its own value, by showing us Germans our own nakedness in a French mirror. But *the* book about Berlin must be free of all journalism. August Endell[7] has employed the only useful method on individual examples in his little book *Die Schönheit der grossen Stadt* (The Beauty of the Big City)[8], which is very much worth reading. But the greater part remains to be done even after Endell: the rhythm of work and pleasure, night and day, freedom and being tied down, high and low, that is to say artistic forms in the choice and arrangements of the impressions. The synthesis must always be left up to the reader. That is how Berlin's development would have it. Only in this way can a work be produced that will be equal in value to Ruederer's[9] *München*[10] and Bahr's *Wien*,[11] a work in which the heart of the great city beats, the symphony in grey, the petrified ocean which has become our homeland.

Originally published as: M.R. Schönlank, "Die Weltstadt Berlin", in: *Nord und Süd*, XXXV, vol. 135, H.6 (2nd December issue, 1910), pp.506–509.

NOTES

1. Raphael is referring to Goethe's "Von deutscher Baukunst" (1772), dedicated to the German architect Erwin von Steinbach (1244–1318), who played an important role in the construction of the Strasbourg Cathedral.

2. Karl Scheffler: Hamburg, 1869 – Überlingen, 1951. German art critic.

3. Karl Scheffler, *Berlin: Ein Stadtschicksal* (Berlin: Reiss, 1910), p.267. Scheffler's emphasis.

4. I.e. the Franco-Prussian war of 1870–1871.

5. Jules Huret: Boulonge-sur-Mer, 1863 – Paris, 1915. Journalist for *l'Écho de Paris* and *Le Figaro*.

6. Jules Huret: *Berlin um Neunzehnhundert*, translated from the French by Nina Knoblich (Albert Langen, Munich, 1909).

7. August Endell: Berlin, 1871 – Berlin, 1925. Jugendstil architect.

8. August Endell, *Die Schönheit der grossen Stadt* (Stuttgart: Strecker & Schröder, 1908).

9. Joseph Anton Heinrich Ruederer: Munich, 1861 – Munich, 1915. Writer.

10. Joseph Ruederer, *München* (Munich: Georg Müller Verlag, 1907).

11. Hermann Bahr, *Wien* (Stuttgart: Krabbe, 1906).

OSSIP DYMOW: THE YOUNGSTER VLAS

Published by Paul Cassirer, Berlin 1910[1]

When I was reading this book I couldn't but be reminded of one of Henri Matisse's paintings. It was a pink surface. On this broad area of background colour, itself gradated, and setting the mood of the whole, a female nude lay diagonally, her flesh also a gradated pink and her contours outlined with sharper modelling brushstrokes. Dymow too writes like this. His is an extraordinary gift, and the scenes, especially those at the end, become very alive, very vital. Still one can perhaps say of this young writer that he has not yet developed the power to combine the individual scenes and images into an equally living whole. I must however say that I have long been interested in this material. When Dymow has the youngster Vlas grow up, he does not present us with the psychology of an adult but rather with the modern child, the inherited nervousness, the awe of everything marvellous and mysterious, an image of the cold, analytic physiological scepticism of those born around 1890, the fruit of the generation of Ibsen, Maeterlinck and Marx.

By turning his attention to Russia, Mr Cassirer has taken a very productive road. One has shown us Americans and Hungarians. Perhaps Mr Cassirer will show us the most interesting artists, the Russians.

Originally published as: M.R. Schönlank, "Ossip Dymow. Der Knabe Wlass", in: *Nord und Süd*, XXXV, vol. 136, H.422 (2nd January issue, 1911), pp.168.

NOTES

1. *Der Knabe Wlas: Ein Roman*, translated into German by Sonja Werner (Berlin: Cassirer, 1910). Ossip Dymow (real name Ossip Issidorowitsch Perelman): Bialystok (Russia; presently Poland), 1878 – New York, 1959. Writer, screen writer, director.

THE NEW SECESSION

Impressionism was at first the psychology of nature. Eyes sated with the brown sauce of the academic studio found an inexhaustible treasure-chest in nature. One was hungry to capture these just discovered delights of air and light in colours, and the acquired facility to see all nuances demanded the manual skill to record them all. One had, in a manner of speaking, acquired the words and the syntax of a new language which could express the impression of every moment, every hour and temperature. One reacted to every perception with an immediate notation, and it happened that by fixing every visible value on the picture surface in a harmony of light colours as the momentary reaction of a temperament, the decorative elements were greatly neglected. One created a series of very valuable exercises in a new many-sided form of expression, but had to let a later generation make great decorative pictures, armed with these means but less tied to the object, to build the house with these newly quarried stones.

A decoration achieved through the colour-perceptions of Impressionism: that is the programme of every country's young artists, i.e. they no longer get their laws from the object. The Impressionist had wished to achieve the impression of the object by means of pure painting; these latter, however, thought of the wall and for the wall and indeed in colours. No longer did they want to reproduce nature in her evanescent appearances, but rather to so concentrate their personal feelings towards the object, compressing them into a characteristic expression, that the expression of their personal feelings is strong enough to become a mural. For a colourful decoration. One places areas of colour side by side, so that these incalculable laws of quantitative colour equilibrium, together with a new freedom of action, will abrogate the rigid scientific laws of qualitative colour. These colour areas do not destroy the basic lines of the represented objects; rather the line is now consciously used as a factor, not expressive of form, not modelling, but descriptive of form, expressing sensation and pinning figural life to the surface. The mere fixing of everything objective to the surface entirely cancels out its significance as reality. Each and every object is just the bearer of a colour, a composition of colours and the whole work is aimed at the impression not of nature, but of sensations. Science and imitation disappear again in favour of re-making.

It is an easy thing to demonstrate that this decorative Impressionism is the logical continuation of the efforts of modern painting. But proving the historical logic of development has never lessened the layman's howl of rage; it has only gradually lent the authority of custom to the older artists. Thus last summer led to an unavoidable split in the Secession. The best of the young artists, the hopeful bearers of a future that is capable of development, have formed themselves into a new Secession. For one could not content oneself with a few phrases, even less with the most dubious attempts at exhibitions which resemble the artificial temperature of greenhouse cultivation, either overheated or ice-cold. One wrapped the young artists in lovely flattering words, in expressions of praise such as 'talent' and 'genius', always hung the worst of the works sent in, or displayed them dreadfully or ripped the coherence of the collection to pieces until one turned them all down. The mutually contradictory introductions of the last two catalogues form a clear expression of their behaviour towards the young artists. One speaks of their puerile technique, the other of promising talents. One speaks of rebels, the other of artists spoiled to the point of modishness.

This alliance was necessary in spite of its fortuitousness. If some critics regard this motley mixture of the most various talents as dubious, the artists believe in the purifying power of time. Just think of the first years of the eleventh century. Did not some of these fall, were they not lost to art? A drab memorial exhibition in the academy, none of these young artists can sink lower than that. It is precisely this fortuitousness which has attracted to the circle temperaments of a completely different nature, in addition to a whole series of representatives of the new thoughts on style, that will guarantee that this new Secession will not itself become the closed association of a school, but the collecting point of all young artists, the place where every new potential will find acceptance. For it never depends on the school or the tendency – they all become conventions, academies, sooner or later – but on the living stream of energy of the artists' ability. As a young student in Strasbourg, Goethe said to the Germans, from the depths of his intuition, everything that can be said about art and which will be a guideline to all these young artists:

'They want you to believe that the fine arts have developed from the inclination which we are supposed to have to beautify the things around us. That is not true. For in the sense that it could be true it would probably be the bourgeois and the craftsman who needed these words, not the philosopher. Art is a long time in the making before it becomes beautiful, and yet is true and great art, yes, often truer and greater than the beautiful itself. For there is a creative nature in man which is seen to come into action as soon as his existence is secured. (…) Now this characteristic art is the only true one. If it produces its effect from inward, unified, personal, independent feeling, unconcerned with, indeed unconscious of everything outside, be it born of the wildest crudity or the most cultivated sensibility, it will be whole and living. You will see countless degrees of this in nations and in individual men. The more the soul is elevated to a feeling for proportions, which alone are beautiful and eternal, the principal harmonies of which can be demonstrate but the mysteries of which one can only feel, and in which alone the life of the God-like genius (…) can frolic, the more this beauty so penetrates the essence of a mind that it seems to have been born with this beauty, that nothing else seems to satisfy it, the happier the artist (…), the more deeply bowed we stand and worship the anointed God.'[1]

Originally published as: M.R. Schönlank, "Die neue Secession", in: *Katalog der Neuen Secession Berlin. 3. Ausstellung: Gemälde; Februar-April, 1911* (Berlin: Baron, 1911).

NOTES

1. Johann Wolfgang von Goethe, "Von deutscher Baukunst" (1772), in: *Goethes Werke* (Hamburger Ausgabe), vol.12, edited by Erich Trunz (Munich: DTV, 1988), pp. 7–15 (p.13ff).

WHITE AND BLACK

The connoisseur joyfully welcomes every exhibition of drawings because here he has the possibility of immediately sensing the artist's psyche, because here the simplest handwriting, the extension of writing with the finger, so to speak, when pencil and charcoal predominate, removes all those veils from the act of creation which are the necessary consequence of a technically complicated material or laborious care. An exhibition of the art of drawing leads directly into the workshop of the psyche of the artist, by showing his most direct utterances.

When in spite of this the exhibition management of the old Secession complains afresh of the poor interest shown by the public, one could derive from this a new element of proof for the once again apparently mislaid thesis that art and the public have no point of contact intellectually. Unfortunately for the management one must admit that the mounting of the exhibition of drawings is technically a most imperfect one. Anyone who feels an intimate relationship to drawing will be frightened off by impossible panes of glass or ugly differences in height (especially in the case of Guys[1]), yet more so, when the artist himself, in the case of the illustrations for example, has counted on a completely different direction of view, a completely different relationship of the single picture to the whole. Is it so difficult to present the drawings in portfolios on stands and at the same time to show the whole book?

In order to exhaustively discuss the aesthetics of an exhibition of drawings one would have to debate the position of drawing within modern art. If I remove etching and every other technique which results in the transformation of objects, their adaptation to its process – one should always have separated the individual techniques in the exhibition – drawing still has a double duty. For one: to fix in itself the impression of nature, or of thought. In this exhibition one gets to know the immediate relationship of the artist's eye to nature, his particular interest in the subject matter, the problems he is currently setting himself, and the level of his ability, his capacity to attain the desired result. For another: the various recordings of nature, working out compositional sketches, registering every stage in the completion of a large work. By showing us the developmental stages, the sequence of drawings makes us see the finished work as the product of strenuous labour and once again how the divine necessity of art is once again born out of chaos, and introduces the only proper relationship between layman and the artist: regard for a great intellectual achievement, respect towards a pre-eminent capacity.

Thus a black and white exhibition should principally always be – granted the admissibility of etchings etc. – a study exhibition in both these senses. That this can be done even by Impressionists was once proved by Liebermann when he showed his *Judengasse*[2] studies in Cassirer's salon. It was the most excellent and instructive impression that I have ever got from Liebermann's art. In the Secession this task has fallen to Hodler. But the hanging commission has robbed the work of most of its effect. The effect of rhythm and natural break should really be so absorbed into the flesh and blood of every artist that such separation of things that belong together and such a linear marshalling should have been perceived as being completely inadequate. Otherwise this room is the most richly satisfying, the most interesting of the exhibition. Hodler's sketches for the *Retreat from Morignano*[3] or *Sensation*[4] enable us to follow his creative method: an experience that has matured my relationship to the way he constructs his accomplished pictures. And since we are given the opportunity to compare Hodler with Rethel[5] on one side and Klimt on the other, we learn not only to value Hodler's great skill as a draughtsman properly, but to recognise that part of it with which this artist, seemingly so alien to the present, pays his tribute to the character of the age. In every one of Hodler's pictures we can discern an element of decadence that can be precisely defined by comparison with Klimt.

Grossman[6] has probably the most outdoor sketches here and, since he is one of those young artists to whom the committee has given a whole wall, it will pay one to have a closer look at him. The subjects which attract this artist are to be found on the outskirts of the metropolis. It is a suburban life, that existence which oscillates between metropolis and village and has developed its own atmosphere of sensuality and corruption. Behind a level pasture we see a towering confusion of tenements. The hurly-burly of a carousel is squeezed into a courtyard. Sickly-coloured cafés with dubious people. A suburban theatre. When one satisfies oneself as to the material that recurs with many of the young artists, one will soon see that the purely artistic charms of these sketches are not very great. If one compares these sketches with, for example, those of similar content by Pechstein in the New Secession, one will not be able to doubt for long where the greater power and the greater capacity lie; Pechstein's intense grasp of the object and responsiveness of hand is so superior that Grossman seems stiff, listless and stammering.

The Secession committee's sober understanding of the present seems to have become romantic and forgetful of the here and now, to be wallowing in past glories and future uncertainties with the romantic solemnity which reveres ancestors and builds golden bridges from the great art of the past to that of the future out of assurances of confidence. In the absence of deeds, words must serve: '(We can) claim with a clear conscience that there are more artistic expressions than ever of talented young individuals, who give us every hope of fruitful maturity in due course.' (From the catalogue.)[7]

The gallery of these ancestors is almost complete and has the merit of not having a dusty effect. These pictures all speak directly. And one shakes one's head: so that was the revolutionary Impressionism, over which the older generation came to blows? Our appreciation of it is already historical, with the question on our lips: and us?

Such was our making: Goya was witness, with his casually-flicked drawings. Delacroix was father, with his sharp eye, for the colours of reality (only his divine imagination is lost. It is good, again to read the praise that Goethe gave to it in connection with the *Faust* lithographs exhibited here.[8] Eckermann noted: 'For the more perfect imaginative powers of such an artist oblige us to consider the situations as being as good as he himself considered them. And if I now must admit that Mr Delacroix has outdone my own vision of scenes that I have created myself, how much more will not the readers find everything alive and going beyond their imaginations!'[9] Daumier, with his caricatures which revealed two worlds, was a sufferer (though the greatness of his vision, the monumentality of his pathos is only rarely preserved) and counterpart to Corot's profound feeling for landscape which, in its immediacy and freshness, far excels that of more recent artists. Then come Manet, Degas, Renoir, the classics of today; finally, the most recent of the French: Pierre Bonnard with lithographs of Paris life and Maurice Denis with lithographs which, with their utterly refined response to sentiment, are completely out of place where they are hung.

The bridge which leads from there to the promising young artists is too shaky all the same; if one is not to do the latter an injustice, it would be better to see them on another day. But even then, in those of them who are allowed to cover whole walls, I cannot see an artistic power strong enough to justify romantic intimations of the future. Nowhere does one feel that powerful stream of artistic potential that awakens hope, even when it has not found adequate expression in the works. Here one can only ask with trepidation when these lights of fashion will be so spoiled that their successors will have to replace them noiselessly.

Hans Meid,[10] who became famous overnight and was honoured with a prize, exhibited in the summer; we can conclude from his pictures that his busy imagination is not matched by his powers of composition. His graphic work, on the other hand, shows his imagination to be a fragment of

Slevogt, his line a graft from other artists. Only time can tell if this road really can lead to a fruitful activity.

As for the rest of the young artists' work that is shown, it can all too often be called Liebermann's, a fact that perhaps says just as much for the leader's strong talent as it does for the lack of power in the young. Between past and future we find a number of worthwhile things embedded; above all, Corinth's drawings and studies. They are of such immediacy and freshness that one follows the artist gladly and, stepping form drawing to drawing, comes closer to him, whereas, presented with his pictures, we remain strangers to him. Meanwhile one finds powerfully imaginative compositional studies and vigorous drawings from nature by Beckmann, Rösler's[11] true to nature landscapes and Pascin's[12] illustrations. Barlach[13] has a room of sculptures and drawings.

Originally published as: M.R. Schönlank, "Weiss und Schwarz", in: *Nord und Süd*, XXXV, vol. 136, H.423 (1st February issue, 1911), pp.241–244.

NOTES

1. Constantin Guys: Vlissingen, 1802 – Paris, 1892. Draughtsman, aquarellist, Crimean War correspondent. Baudelaire called him 'the painter of modern life'.

2. Max Liebermann. *Judengasse in Amsterdam*. 1908. Oil on canvas. 74 x 63 cm. Städelsches Kunstinstitut, Frankfurt am Main.

3. Ferdinand Hodler. *Rückzug von Marignano*. Designs for the frescoes in the Schweizerischen Landesmuseum, Zürich, 1896-1899.

4. Ferdinand Hodler. *Empfindung I*. 1901/2. Oil on canvas. 193 x 280.5 cm. Private collection; *Empfindung II*. 1901/2. Oil on canvas. 120 x 171 cm. Private collection (fam. Schmidheiny).

5. Alfred Rethel: Diepenbenden (presently Aachen), 1816 – Düsseldorf, 1859. Painter, draughtsman.

6. Rudolph Grossmann: Freiburg im Breisgau, 1882 – Freiburg im Breisgau, 1941. Painter, graphic artist. Member of the Berlin Secession.

7. "Vorwort", in *Katalog der einundzwanzigsten Ausstellung der Berliner Secession: Zeichnende Künste*, exhibition catalogue (Berlin, 1910), pp. 9–11 (p.10).

8. Eugène Delacroix, 17 lithographs for Goethe's *Faust*, 1826.

9. Johann Peter Eckermann, *Conversations with Goethe*, Wednesday, 29th November, 1826.

10. Hans Meid: Pforzheim, 1863 – Ludwigsburg, 1957. Painter, graphic artists, book illustrator. Member of the Berlin Secession from 1911.

11. Waldemar Rösler: Striesen, 1882 – Arys, 1916. Landscape painter, graphic artist.

12. Jules Pascin (real name Julius Mordecai Pinkas): Vidin (Bulgaria), 1885 – Paris, 1930. Painter, graphic artist.

13. Ernst Barlach: Wedel, 1870 – Rostock, 1938. Expressionist sculptor, graphic artist, poet.

THE ACADEMY AND THE NEW ARTISTS' ASSOCIATION

A grey day, heavy as lead. He was so tired that he didn't know whether to sleep or stay awake. In the Academy were neither people nor pictures. Just the wide emptiness of the great rooms. Like a poison that silences active reserves, sucks the life out of the bones and sends one to sleep. Soon I was so listless that I could not bring myself to leave. As I found a mixture of Klinger[1] in sugar, Sunday family magazine and lemonade in Room 6, which, under the name of Meyer, Hans: *A Dance of Death* covered several walls, I slid into a chair.

Accompanied by an old lady, a pair of shaking knees shuffled into the room.

'I have a wretched cold in my head. What shall I do?'

'Have a warm lemonade,' said the wrinkled old dear, 'you'll see, it'll work.'

'Very good, very good. Deep, that!'

'Meyer, Hans: A Dance of Death.'

'Perhaps I have the flu as well.'

'Limode. And then a good sweat.'

Then he tottered out on his stick. Somebody tugged me and I awoke.

'The Michelangelo and Victoria Colonna[2] of German criticism. But don't upset yourself, he's dead.'

'O…'

'Yes, omega. Somebody's already written him a swansong, the sweating cure won't help much. By the way, I'm Youth.'

'Stop boasting. You don't have to be so pushy with your symbolism.'

But I couldn't quieten the little chap. He pulled me away with him. In his hurry, he took a picture and three busts out of the room with him. He played football with the heads across the courtyard, through the gate and on through the Zoo to Cassirer's salon.

'Oh… ah.'

'Ah… oh, I'm Youth.'

'Don't brag.'

He ducked for an instant as I showed him a few mediocre pictures.

'Dilettantism is everywhere. Incidentally: La femme.'

He was right. And now I had to let him lead me. What he showed me was youth. The great aim: a purely painterly decoration. The artistic energy of the most various individuals.

A great vista. A tremendous stream of living energy that went straight to the spectator, augmented the power of the eyes and the faculty of comprehension to a rare degree of vitality. That is our art, that is us.

'So-o', asked the little fellow; and now listen to him: 'This exhibition would only be justified if it was a *carnival joke* played by Munich artists to make fun of certain snobbish circles in Berlin. It would be a well thought out joke and a brilliantly executed one. Seriously, its' the most *extraordinary cheek* that we've ever witnessed. These sculptures and paintings with their horrific distortions seem the monstrous birth of madness, the...'

'Enough, I know how...'

Suddenly, the lad had a bow in his hand and drew his arrow onto a tight string. There was no way I could mistake the movement.

'The *old fellow*? Come, now!'

'No, the *old*!'

Originally published as: M.R. Schönlank, "Akademie und neue Künstlervereinigung", in: *Der Sturm*, vol.49 (February 4, 1911), p.392.

NOTES

1. Max Klinger: Leipzig, 1857 – Grossjena bei Naumburg, 1920. Painter, graphic artist, sculptor.

2. Vittoria Colonna: Castello di Marino, 1492 – Rome, 1547. One of the most popular poets of 16th- century Italy.

CURT HERRMANN: THE STRUGGLE FOR STYLE

Published by Erich Reiss, Berlin, 1911

In recent years one has often emphasised, with a condescension paternalistic in its offensiveness, that theory always means a decline or a faltering in productive power, and supported this dubious wisdom with a sentence from Goethe's warehouse of quotations, without considering what art-historical value-judgements this sentence would entail were it to prove to be true.

Every artist consciously creates according to certain definite principles, and that modern artists also express themselves on this subject is only a happy indication of a self-assured culture. And who should have more valuable things to say about his own art than the artist himself, who is often all the more moved by it than is anyone else? Who better to lead us to that border where all speech becomes redundant and feeling begins? One can extend this praise to Mr Herrmann: that he brings the reader into intimate contact with his art, i.e. to that of Neo-Impressionism. It is astounding that one can hear of technical games where one finds so much feeling and greatness of desire.

Psychologists have often brought up the sceptical question of the value of books by artists. I think that their use is only a question of feel. We must make allowances to the artist as creator for any one-sidedness, but it's all the much more elegant when this is avoided, as it is here. Herrmann does not see in Neo-Impressionism the one sovereign road to art. What I would particularly like to reckon to his account is his emphasis that art is a goal to which different paths lead. His, that of Matisse, and yet other ones. It's no use presenting Impressionism as the last phase, the *non plus ultra*, as one likes to do in certain circles today. The Holy Spirit is eternal movement and the young, too, are on their way to art. On a way different from that of the Impressionists, but with the same artistry and vitality.

One must judge the publishers less favourably than the artist. One simply may not bind in so many blank pages which cannot but distract one from one's reading. The choice of illustrative material is also deficient. If Mr Reiss, as he seems to, really wants to fill the gap in our publishing system so keenly felt by the young visual artists, then it must be done in better style. The need was certainly a crying one.

Originally published as: M.R. Schönlank, "Curt Herrmann: Der Kampf um den Stil", in: *Nord und Süd*, XXXV, vol. 136, H.424 (2nd February issue, 1911), pp.355.

NOTES

1. Curt Herrmann: Merseburg, 1854 – Erlangen, 1929. Painter, founding member of the Berlin Secession.

THE NEW SECESSION

One could use a celestial metaphor: God the Father, the Son, and the Holy Spirit are present at every exhibition. Most visibly the Son, the incarnate revelation of the Father, the artistic energy of the creative master condensed to matter, and the Holy Spirit – woe to the exhibition in every room of which he does not rule; he, the eternally-young, perpetually moving one who, ungraspable in his infinity, has shown himself in the most manifold variations in the course of history, without losing anything of the fullness and richness of the beginning! Then one would have nothing to say about an exhibition to the few initiates of art, for the Father also lives in the Son, the artist in the work, as one may read: the Father is in me.

On the occasion of the New Secession exhibition I would like to write about the artistic type, because it seems to me that a new generation lies behind these works, one that is completely different from the older one. One will not only come to understand that the conflict between the Old and the New Secessions is a necessary one, but also achieve a positive attitude towards pictures which have been ridiculed beyond all measure.

The new generation is the heir of the older. That which an unfettered individualism has created and conquered with an astonishing fecundity and rich confusion will have to be taken up and re-experienced in its total breadth by them, in order to try and shape a new life from it. Marx's social-revolutionary tendencies in the form of social sympathy or in master-race aristocracy had blurred the social gradations, undervalued as they were in the worth of their living strength, and robbed man of the social organism's compulsion. Ibsen's physiological scepticism had generated a nervy impatience of psychic lumber, pathos, and other mendacities of life, so that an increased self-knowledge, a sharpened self-observation deprived one of any firm inner ground. One indulged in an orgy of rummaging doubt that ripped every veil from the mysteries and yet found its counterpart in Maeterlinck's symbolism, in the anxiety and the longing to worship the unknown of the twilight, not to be dragged out into the light of day.

If development were to be at all possible then the following generation had to take this burden upon itself joyfully, to affirm it exultantly; that is, they had to fuse it inwardly in their experience and, out of the many antitheses produced by analysis, to create a new unified structure: from the stones, the building. Hence in every area of intellectual activity the mask of this generation is *synthesis*. It is only a variation on the same theme when one hears scientists speak of a renaissance of the sciences, of the function of sociology and biology, the doing away with specialisation, or when visual artists fight for a pure painterly style, against Impressionism and for decoration. Everywhere we have, instead of the endless collecting of *visual hints*, a self-sufficient intellectual endeavour, which has already given a new ring to the despised words 'obstruction', 'system' and 'composition'.

The essence of synthesis in painting would be precisely understood in the approach that scorns to fix the fleeting impression, the irrecoverably lost movement of the instant. 'I prefer to take the risk of losing the individual stimulus by emphasising the character of the landscape. To make up for it I gain more stability. Behind the sequence of moments that constitute the ephemeral existence of essence and things and lends them their mutable forms of experience, one can look for a truer, more essential character to which the artist will cleave, so as to give a more enduring interpretation of reality' (Matisse[1]), and under the motto '*plus de stabilité*' one strives for the unity of form and colour.

To the degree that, in the art of creation, human activity has developed in its intellectual aspect especially, the artist has an increasing feeling for the activity of his own personality. Impressionism and the science contemporary with it were characterised by a devotion to nature that one must call passion to the highest degree. One lost oneself in nature, one yielded oneself up so penetratingly to it that it explains the immediacy of this naturalism and the mysticism of the object-reproduction and the most immaterial of colours. One sought to blur abstraction, the condition for every plastic art, by depriving the unyielding evidence of the eyes of its effect in each and every sensuous area, and tried thereby to come close to the impression of nature. A passivity characterised by an unheard-of *receptivity* of all the senses has a correspondingly *active intellectuality* which – affirmative of the nervous sensory receptivity – does not reproduce sensory impressions in order to re-awaken the feeling of the impression, but rather tries to form them for expressive purposes.

One of the first marks of this intellectual activity is the tendency to *simplicity*. One has done any amount of damage in this time with the concept of the 'primitive'. Here we see most clearly how very much this young generation is the heir of the last. Their primitive is the complexity of Impressionism concentrated and condensed. The primitive is nothing childlike, naïve or unconscious, but rather a synthesis, a simplification in which all the elements of the highest sensory stimulation and the tautest self-knowledge tremble in living concert – even if increasingly instinctively. This is a struggle of overcoming, not of denial. A saying like André Gide's 'a great man has only one concern: to become as human as possible, let us say indeed, as banal as possible, and – O wonder! – from this struggle he creates his individual personality', is only after all possible when one has gone through Baudelaire's 'la sensibilité de chacun c'est son génie.'[2]

A second mark of this activity is *clarity*. Gauguin was the first to claim it as a title of fame. Since then it has been a law of the artist that everything has to be spread out on the surface clearly, that the picture has to have as great a visibility as possible. Concerning the value of this obligation for the artist, Maurice Denis[3] writes: 'If we wish that his feeling be subject to the judgement of the understanding, then we surely hope that these constraints will augment his abilities and that his genius, held in check by just rules, will thereby gain greater concentration, strength, and profundity. We are right to be tired of the individualistic spirit, the culmination of which is to throw every tradition, every doctrine, every discipline overboard and to regard the artist as a kind of demigod, for whom rule is replaced by whim.'[4]

We can see from the transformation of the word pathos as a term of value with what rigorous inward struggle one has wrested this feeling of activity. It seemed to include everything that an Impressionist – I mean always Impressionism as worldview – hated out of the depths of his soul: the conventional empty movement, the self-deceiving demand of the ideal, the gesture turned sour in the academy, the dusty social lie; everything, in short, that was not soberly bourgeois, shorn of sounding phrases, boring. It seemed impossible ever again to speak of a high pathos; the word seemed forever hollow. And yet it was into just this despised expression that the young artists poured their burgeoning joy in artistic activity, a joy before which they had occasionally trembled as if before a mendacious phantom. Pathos had once again become creative joy that affirms everything that is, because it shapes it. It is an anti-bourgeois feeling, because it is a creative one.

'To carry together into one what is fragment in mankind and riddle and horrid accident – as poet, riddle guesser and redeemer of chance I taught them to work on the future, and to creatively redeem everything that was.' (Nietzsche, *Zarathustra*, "On Old and New Tablets").[5]

One can already see from these indications that the artists of the 'New Secession' represent a new generation. It was good in principle to say at the opening that one works under the compulsion of one's personality and one's time. There are very appropriate words of Henri Matisse: 'All artists bear the mark of their time, but the greatest ones are those who have let themselves be stamped most deeply by it. Whether we like it or not, and much as we would like to emphasise that we are refugees in this age, it still produces a solidarity between itself and us from which none of us can escape.'[6]

Originally published as: M.R. Schönlank, "Die neue Secession", in: *Nord und Süd*, XXXV, vol. 137, H.427 (1st April issue, 1911), pp.70–73.

NOTES

1. Henri Matisse, "Notes d'un peintre", in: *La Grande Revue*, December 1908. Published in German as "Notizen eines Malers", in: *Kunst und Künstler*, VII, Issue 8 (May 1909), pp.335–347 (p.340).

2. 'A person's sensibility is his genius'. The quote is from Baudelaire's *Fusées*, XVII (1897). Published in German in 1909 as: *Raketen: Tagebücher*, translated by Erich Oesterheld (Berlin: Oesterheld, 1909).

3. Maurice Denis: Granville, 1870 – Saint-Germain-en-Laye, 1943. Painter. Founding member of the post-Impressionist group Les Nabis.

4. Maurice Denis, "Cézanne", in: *L'Occident*, 68 (September, 1907).

5. Friedrich Nietzsche, *Thus Spoke Zarathustra* (1883–1885), III, "On Old and New Tablets", 3 (1884), translated by Adrian Del Caro (Cambridge: Cambridge U.P., 2006). Nietzsche's emphasis.

6. Henri Matisse, see note 1, p.347.

THE NEW PAINTING. THE NEW SECESSION

Not only was the strength of Impressionism tightly bound to the motif of the landscape, but its aesthetics emphasised again and again that its roots lay, in defiance of all convention, in its direct relationship with nature, in its closeness to it: the task and aim of this painting is to approximate to the impression of nature. Nature was unfiltered art as soon as one abstracted it with the painter's means. Once one had found the motif, intellectual activity was confined to the composition of the colours: everything else was left to chance. It would be banal to regard this verism as a poor copy of nature and to compare it with photography. But once alerted by the authoritative sentence, 'Nature is a goose, first we must make something out of her', one will, *ad hoc*, recognise in this tenet of Impressionism too, merely a relative, pointed formulation, the general validity of which is easy to shake when one examines the relationship of nature to visual art. Leopold Ziegler[1] has analysed the gulf between them most acutely in a significant essay in *Logos*. He denies that there is any community of feeling or of mood between them. We apprehend nature as *that which is* with all our organs of sense;

the harmony of all these sensory apprehensions awakens the mood of Pan. Or we invest them with human feelings and see then an allegory of our soul. 'Because of this twofold causation the mood is non-painterly, that is to say, poetic or musical, as well as extra-painterly, that is, founded in other than optical-spatial impressions.'[2] We sense nature in its eternal changing as the 'analogy of one of the works of time (...), hence one is a visual artist precisely to the extent that one can, in place of the *eternal* state of affairs, put the *enduring* object which one creates artificially, since neither nature nor experience offers it to him.'[3] One can no more assert the harmony of objects among one another than one can the community of feeling, for the work of artistic creation has come from nature by way of a number of activities which must alter the object in some way or another, in order to make art out of nature.

Naturally no aesthetic formulation, be it even so perspicuous, can set the value of an art at nought. Neither do I direct myself at the masterpieces of Impressionism, which like every art are beyond all value-judgements, but at aesthetic dogma. There can be the most various relationships between nature and creative power besides the one that is preached, that of slavish clinging. In former ages one derived one's conceptions from the individual object by means of linear abstraction. This the Impressionist did without, because he wished to represent the object in relation to air and light. Why shouldn't there be other new forms beyond this possibility as well? For the artists of the New Secession *sensation* is now the element determining form, so that it is no longer closeness to nature but the expression of feeling that is the aim of their work. By this is not intended that sentiment of whichever artist one comes to think of, which usually comes into play before the act of observation, foils its development and prevents its ripening. Here, however, the artist seeks to form a colour-composition out of the first thing in the visible world of appearances that arouses feeling in him, so that nature leaps out again; not, however, as a phenomenal value, an augmented and clarified observation, a piece of the psychology of nature accidentally caught in the picture-frame, but as a self-contained picture of her essence and her character, under the condition of the complete annihilation of the object's significance through the medium of the artist; a concentrated, abstracted expression.

'There are two ways to express things,' says Matisse, 'one is brutally to show them, the other is to summon them up through art. By getting away from the literal representation of movement one attains to more beauty and greatness (...) It is not possible for me to slavishly copy nature; I am obliged to interpret her and to subordinate her to the *spirit of the picture*. When I have discovered all the relationships of my colour-tones, a living concord of colour must result from this, a harmony analogous to that of a musical composition.'[4]

If one wished briefly and pointedly to formulate the process of artistic expression and the position of nature in both movements, one could say: in Impressionism, impersonal devotion and personal reproduction dominate; among the young stylists, personal devotion and impersonal reproduction. Maurice Denis, who belongs only conditionally to this group, only when one abstracts sufficiently, writes:

'From the standpoint of subjectivity the thought "nature seen through a temperament"[5] is replaced by the theory of the equivalent, a symbol. We formulated the law that the feelings or spiritual states caused by a certain event provide the artist with signs or plastic equivalents which enable him to reproduce these feelings or spiritual states without having to counterfeit the actual drama; that our emotions must at every stage have a corresponding harmony in reality which enables us to translate them. Art is no longer a sensation which we absorb with our eyes (...) no, it is the creation of our intellect, to which nature has only given the coincidental prompting. "Instead of working with the eyes, we apprehend with the mysterious centre of *thought*", as Gauguin said (...) and art (...) became the subjective transformation of nature.

Seen from the objective standpoint, decorative, aesthetic and rational composition – to which the Impressionists attached no importance, opposing to it their preference for improvisation – (...) became the necessary note of amelioration to the theory of equivalents. Just as this theory permitted all interpretation, even to the point of caricature, all exaggeration of character, so the objective transformation required the artist to turn everything into beauty. In short: the expressive synthesis, the symbol of a sensation had now to be reproduced by a penetrating description and at the same time be a work of art pleasing to the eye.'[6]

With these last words the aim of the new movement is elucidated: the closed composition. Whereas for the Impressionists picture-format and representation did not stand in any obligatory necessary relationship to one another and the surface was indeterminate in its size, just as content was a section taken out at will from the eternal stream of appearances, a new law now emerges, one as immovable as bronze. Those artists who think by means of and for the wall compose under the coercion of the picture surface also, so that an enlargement or reduction is impossible. For every surface-area one must conceive anew. Apart from the format, the surface itself compels. Everything of the object must stay in the surface. Spatial composition is eliminated. On this surface the colours are flat, evenly painted out and, insofar as they describe objects, nailed to the surface with a contour line. This line, occasionally black, *more often* a contrast in tone or colour, has become a painterly means and a powerfully expressive marking in its elasticity and richness of content. It does not create form, but rather circumscribes it, expresses sensation.

The perceptions of colour with which these young artists calculate stem entirely from the achievements of their predecessors. Since the Impressionists' reproduction of nature never was a photographic copy of it but the artistic psychology of the painterly values in appearances, they brought the painter's means to a refinement of nuance undreamt of until then, one that will be their distinction for ever. An unparalleled sensibility – 'la sensibilité de chacun c'est son génie',[7] in Baudelaire's excellent characterisation – makes one receptive to the finest nuancing of every sensory phenomenon, forces the hand to reproduce every differentiation in sensory perception and squeezes the expression of perceptions deriving from other sensory areas out of the hard, dead vehicle of paint. 'Doubtless the young man can't paint but one somehow *smells* the sea from his work; and none of the proper painters manage that', said a sea-captain about Whistler. And the victory over matter had an intoxicating effect; one formulated art by formulating the laws of matter. Van de Velde[8] laid it down in the following sentences: 1. All matter develops step by step towards life... The first trace of beauty coincides with the first trace of life in matter… Thought never fertilised the matter in which picture, statue, or poem has become real. 2. All matter develops step by step towards its most immaterial form of appearance.

The truth of this second *law* immediately subtilised the artists' intention beyond the physical. One wanted – at least in theory – to have the strongest colours possible, but instead ended up by giving a blond, bright cast to the picture which deprived the colours of the sharpness of local tone. Colour was reciprocally sublated.

The contrast between the colour-perceptions of the young artists and those of the Impressionists can be expressed in Fechner's[9] formula: the differences between stimuli are reduced in inverse proportion to their intensities. Because one wishes colour to express, one dispenses with its minute division and optical mixing. One prefers – deliberately to increase the materiality of the paint – the dark, saturated colours of the spectrum, and paints them out in large masses. The Impressionists emphasised the qualities of colour and tried to establish the laws of their relationships scientifically. One could leave the balancing of the colour-masses to a not always felicitous instinct because, compared to the picture-area, they were divided up into minimal areas. The agglomeration of colour-particles into areas of colour gave rise to two new problems: the relationship of form and colour and the balancing of the colour-masses. The artistic instinct, which was in danger of being trapped by Neo-Impressionism in a scientific thesis which was not even certain, found in these quantitative calculations expressive possibilities of a sort most individual and capable of variation.

One has wished to believe – even the otherwise so sober and unaffected Liebermann in his aphoristic epilogue – that this totally new movement is merely a lion-skin affected by young people who can do nothing. And contemporary criticism, as unashamed as only the most profoundly impotent can be, has revealed a most shocking incomprehension. One is once again bankrupt with aesthetic formulas and now with breathtakingly shameless leadenness declares the young artists to be idiots. Completely unable to regard works of art as the expression of a full, strong and energetically streaming power of artistic creation, they fail to recognise the seriousness and the strenuous, laborious efforts of the artists. One overlooks the immense breadth of this movement, which is long at home in literature and is about to conquer the theatre. This is not whim, but conviction, and the battle is fought under that banner.

Originally published as: A.R. Schönlank [sic], "Die neue Malerei. Neue Secession", in: *Der Sturm*, vol.58 (April 8, 1911), pp.463–464.

NOTES

1. Leopold Ziegler: Karlsruhe, 1881 – Überlingen, 1958. Philosopher.

2. Leopold Ziegler, "Ueber das Verhältnis der bildenden Künste zur Natur", in: *Logos, Internationale Zeitschrift für Philosophie der Kultur*, vol. 1 (1910/11), pp.95–124 (p.105).

3. *Ibid.*, p.105ff; Raphael cites somewhat freely here.

4. Henri Matisse, see note 1 on page 95. Raphael's emphasis.

5. 'A work of art is a corner of nature viewed through a temperament.' Emile Zola, *Mes haines* (originally published 1866).

6. Maurice Denis, "Von Gauguin und van Gogh zum Klassizismus", in: *Kunst und Künstler*, VIII, 2 (November, 1909), pp.86-101 (pp.92–94).

7. 'A person's sensibility is his genius'. See note 2 on page 95.

8. Henry van de Velde: Antwerp, 1863 – Zürich, 1957. Painter, architect, art critic.

9. Gustav Theodor Fechner: Gross Särchen, 1801 – Leipzig, 1887. Philosopher, physicist, experimental psychologist.

THE "NEW SECESSION" IN BERLIN

Impressionism was at first the psychology of nature. Eyes sated with the brown sauce of the academic studio found a treasure-chest of values in nature. One was hungry to capture the just-discovered delights of air and light in colours, and the acquired facility to see all nuances demanded the manual skill to record them all. Perception and reaction were separated by so brief an instant that the decorative elements of the picture had to be greatly neglected. Thus the gains of Impressionism were to be found less in the works themselves than in the new colour-scale abstracted from its renderings of nature.

A decoration achieved through the colour perception of Impressionism: that is the programme of every country's young artists, i.e. they no longer get their laws from the object. The Impressionists had wished to achieve the impression of the object by means of pure painting; they, however, think of the wall, and for the wall, and that in colour. The figuration is emphasised by the background of broad areas of colour, it always stays in the surface as if held there by an outline that does not express form or model it but rather describes it, characterises the impression, and keeps life bound to the surface. Dividing up the colour masses, balancing them: these very subjective, incalculable relationships among colour-quantities and this line are the artist's means of achieving a decoration in pure colour. The object as such is naturally quite unimportant and is merely the bearer of colour and compositional values.

It is an easy thing to demonstrate that this decorative Impressionism is the logical continuation of the efforts of modern painting. Niemeyer has attempted to pursue the historical development: 'Impressionism was superseded by the style of Cézanne, the logical extension of Manet's optical syntheses which, after the atmospherical absolutism of landscape art, once again taught one to understand painting as the pure creation of colour. His art (...) presented the new generation with the problem of conglomerating the inconceivable sum of the optical faces of nature into colour surfaces which are clear and simple and suffused with the breath of the most delicate contrasts, of comprehending the functional unity of bodily appearance, air and space as a closed system of colour values (...) In its massively sculptural structure and its simplification of form, Cézanne's painting signifies the reaction of the deepest Roman feeling against the clear, more northerly manner of Impressionism, with its subtle analysis of optical phenomena. If the latter style reflected the multiplicity and movement of all nature with its manifold splitting up of colour and its rapid, momentary application of paint, then Cézanne's picture responds to the impression of nature with the unity of floating colours. After Cézanne, Matisse has most recently gained influence on artistic youth by extracting the linear essence from Cézanne's sculptural constructions.'[1]

But proving the historical logic of development has never lessened the layman's howl of rage; it has only gradually lent the authority of custom to the older artists. Thus it had to come to a split in the Secession last summer. The best of the young artists, the hopeful bearers of a future capable of development, have formed themselves into a new secession because they had been suddenly deprived of the opportunity to exhibit which they had long enjoyed. This group of evicted artists does not consist only in representatives of the new thoughts on style such as Pechstein, Kirchner, Schmidt-Rottluff, Nolde and Heckel. The chance circumstances of its formation have brought two lyricists into the circle: Melzer[2] and Müller-Steglitz;[3] these circumstances have also made the New Secession into the collecting-point for young artists in general, into the place where every young potential will find a welcome.

Originally published as: M.R. Schönlank, "Die 'Neue Secession' in Berlin", in: *Bildende Küstler*, I, vol.4 (April? 1911), p.155–156.

NOTES

1. Wilhelm Niemeyer, "Vorrede", in: *Ausstellung des Sonderbundes westdeutscher Kunstfreunde und Künstler. Düsseldorf 1910*, exhibition catalogue (Düsseldorf, 1910), pp.7–16

2. Moriz Melzer: Albendorf, Böhmen, 1877 – Berlin, 1966. Painter, graphic artist. Founding member of the New Secession.

3. I.e. Otto Mueller: Liebau (presently, Lubawka, Poland), 1874 – Breslau (presently Wroclaw, Poland), 1930. Painter, graphic artist. Member of Die Brücke from 1910.

LIEBERMANN'S GOOD SAMARITAN

Since Impressionism freed painting from the shackles of a prosy and conventional academicism and brought the painter's means of representation to a perfection autonomous virtuosity through a subtle study of nature, a new generation of artists has given itself a new aim: the picture. The Impressionists rebutted the charge that their pictures were only sketches with the completely admissible comparison with Meissonier, a reference which underlined the superiority of their own illusionist, allusive procedure. It is not, however, the procedure but the aim I have in mind when I say that their canvases are not pictures but only fragments of pictures.

It is my belief that even the conception of a picture is different from the initial stages of any work which has not succeeded in breaking its relationship of model and copy to nature or to the creator. In its design, the picture proceeds from a whole. Before the artist can begin to record his sensation it must have been so long shaped and modelled in him that a completeness, a picture, has emerged from the fullness and multiplicity of natural impressions and visual images, that from now on determines every single form from within itself, from its life and existence. One needs to have overcome both nature and oneself, to have formed out of the play of both a third element, something new, that was not there before: the picture, the clear, visual total conception; one must now subordinate to it every natural form and every connection with personal experience in order to derive from it the justification, transformation or rejection of each and every motif. This is why I think that every Naturalism is incapable of picture-creation. For in its work it sticks to the individual natural forms, it justifies its representational procedure by the natural truth of personal apprehension; it cannot subordinate its representation to a total conception, since the totality first appears in the finished product, the solution that results from the summation of independently co-existing parts and details.

But by basing his picture-creation on a total conception, the artist becomes a free creator from a certain moment in the creative process. As soon as he has condensed the sensation to a total conception, as soon as the principal masses, lines colours and lights have sorted themselves out in his intellect, he can work consciously and freely at giving these main bearers the strongest possible expression. After he has formed the experience between the conscious and the unconsciousness, he will now be able as an adept to work out, so to speak, the clearest, most emphatic and yet simplest effect. If he knows what principal lines are called for he will be able to strengthen them with another curvature. The same applies to colour and light. The artist can strengthen here, weaken there with no regard for, or consideration of nature or for fixed connections, just as it seems called for by the harmony and life of the whole. For he no longer derives his laws from nature, but from the picture. The picture, however, is something stable, a situation, so to speak – the contrary of all tendencies of movement and time of the Impressionists. And here we seem to have the deepest aesthetic foundation of a fact, the reality of which has been demonstrated anew by Liebermann's *Good Samaritan*.[1]

Liebermann has for years fought doggedly for picture-creation. One has attributed his failure to his subject-matter, his keeping to legends with which our age feels no affinity. But the story of *Samson and Delilah*, as well as the parable of the Good Samaritan, are of such wide, universal expressiveness that they can absorb and bring out the modern sensibility also. Their form is so great that it can take on any version of the theme, no matter how novel. I read the passage in Luke:

'Who is thy neighbour?

Jesus answered and spoke: 'There was a man who went from Jerusalem down towards Jericho and fell among murderers; they stripped him and beat him and left him lying half dead.

And it happened that a priest came that way; and when he saw him, he passed him by.

It was the same with a Levite, that he saw him and went his way.

A Samaritan, however, came along on his journey and when he saw him he was moved to pity; he came to him, bound up his wounds and poured oil and wine on them and took him up on his beast, carried him to the inn and cared for him.

The next day he continued on his journey and took out two pence and gave them to the landlord and said to him: take care of him. What you do over and above this, I will pay to you on my return.

Who of the three was neighbour to him who fell among murderers, do you think?'

He said: 'he who showed mercy to him.'[2]

The so godless XVIth century (Veronese) and the pantheistic XVIIth century (Rembrandt) created their pictures on the basis of this parable, and I see nothing in it to prevent the artist of the XIXth (sic!)[3] century from representing the social sympathy of his century through it. It is not the subject-matter but the Impressionist tendency to destroy the real life of things in favour of the varying moments of the atmosphere; a transferral to the history-painting: one must turn the spiritual into a still-life. And so Liebermann gives us, instead of the demeanour of this century's social feeling, a simple but boring still-life, spiritless and unoriginal, for it reminds us of the – even a few years ago one would have said academic – Pietà compositions.

But let us leave the literary and deal with the picture. It cannot be denied that the artist – especially compared to the second version of the Delilah picture[4] – has made progress towards the picture. One clearly sees the conceptual coherence with the Brandenburg landscape and admires the resolute simplification and cutting-down into large areas. One sees how the individual tree-trunks are positioned entirely in relation to the figures. But that doesn't stop the foreground, with its Italian flatness, from falling out of the picture or prevent the figure-groups from being two separate, unconnected parts, nor does it prevent the high total tone of the picture from being too brightly pitched for the subject-matter; the right-hand background with its advancing man from being pettily picturesque as a story and counter-productively expressive as a tonal passage; the simplified areas of colour from being meagre and tedious in their effect. All that remains are certain piquancies in the purely artistic element, which one enjoys much more acutely in his self-portrait,[5] and of which Slevogt is the brilliant exponent at this exhibition. His pictures bear witness to a fine culture of painting. They show what an adept can draw out from painting through his command of technique. Whoever gives himself up willingly to the pursuit of virtuosity can even unlearn the *métier* of intellectually arid portraiture (can there really be such mindless people?). This cultivation of ability is the surest and most appropriate storehouse of Impressionist art, one which the young artists should bring into their work to as great an extent as their compositional ideal will allow. Their love of colour seems to me to suppress richness of tone as well as intensity of expression. With their links to the tradition of Corot, the French artists seem to be in advance of our own. But Pechstein's own gifts, apart from the failure of Liebermann, have given the clearest justification of his tendencies and personality, whatever shape his career may take.

When one goes through the rooms of the old Secession one is astonished at how quickly and how rightly one has accustomed oneself to the epithet 'old'. One does not become any younger when one prescribes oneself a dose of stale *so-called* Expressionists from Paris, a painter of kitsch like Manguin,[6] who belongs in the Lehrter Bahnhof,[7] an Othon Friesz,[8] whom one can only describe as an adulteration of Cézanne for the poor in mind, weak efforts from Puy[9] and Marquet![10] All that is left is de Vlaminck and the youthful works of Picasso; one does not become younger when one writes about a national German artistic youth and can show no more than a hopeless reality (apart from Bondy[11] and Pascin). Mister Corinth should not write that, should not write at all; he betrays that his mind has become academic, or that it always was, and invokes words in my memory which come from Apollinaire's satirical pen:

'L'ignorance et la frénésie, voilà bien les caractéristiques de l'impressionisme.'[12]

Originally published as: M.R. Schönlank, "Liebermanns barmherziger Samariter", in: *Nord und Süd*, XXXV, vol. 138, H.435 (1st August issue, 1911), pp.210–212.

NOTES

1. Max Liebermann. *The good Samaritan*. 1911. Oil on canvas. 93 x 111 cm. Wallraf-Richartz-Museum, Cologne.

2. Luke, 10: 29-37.

3. Max Liebermann, *Samson and Delilah*. 1902. Oil on canvas. 150 x 212 cm. Städelsches Kunstinstitut, Frankfurt am Main.

4. Raphael means the XXth century.

5. Max Liebermann. *Der Künstler mit Zigarette* (The Artist with a Cigarette). 1909. Oil on canvas. 113 x 93 cm. Kunsthalle, Hamburg.

6. Henri-Charles Manguin: Paris, 1874 – St. Tropez, 1949. Fauvist painter.

7. Exhibition building near Berlin's Lehrter Bahnhof (train station, closed 1951; since 2006, the site of Berlin's Hauptbahnhof).

8. Achille-Émile Othon Friesz: Le Havre, 1879 – Paris, 1949. Fauvist painter.

9. Jean Puy: Roanne, 1976 – Paris, 1949. Fauvist painter.

10. Albert Marquet: Bordeaux, 1875 – Paris, 1947. Fauvist painter.

11. Walter Bondy: Prague, 1880 – Toulon, 1940. Painter, gallerist.

12. 'Ignorance and craziness, these are the characteristics of Impressionism.'

EXPRESSIONISM

In the thirteenth issue of *Pan*, mister Lovis Corinth has published a study under the title "The Latest Painting", in which he seeks to write off young artists as a horde of imitators. They imitate Cézanne (about whom mister Corinth writes as academically as one should about him), van Gogh and Gauguin. They copy 'the present-day pictures of Negroes and Malayans, the painting on Indian tepees.' In short, 'the young forget that no master has ever fallen from the sky, and that everything great has come into being through taking pains, through work, and through learning. They begin – as Liebermann rightly says – where the great masters have left off.'[1]

Behind these truisms is concealed the usual accusation of inability that is levelled at every new phenomenon. The art historian finds in it a rich vein of scholarship, mister Corinth himself suffered under it and now passes it on as proudly as any academy teacher. Regarded psychologically, this accusation conceals the incomprehension of that which one has had the impertinence to condemn out of hand. For, to the comprehending mind, all these so-called defects are transformed into necessities, into intentions – providing of course, that we have before us the gifts and ability of a Matisse.

One can judge an old or a new art, not by the yardstick of absolute ability but by that of a relative willing. And as soon as one asks about the younger generation's will to art, everything that mister Corinth calls inability reveals itself as the willing of a purpose. Admittedly this will is different from that of the Impressionists. It is a new, emerging art and its differences with Impressionism will at some stage need to be elaborated, so that in the future only ill-will or academicism can speak of a dilettantism of ability.

But first I must break the bad habit which tries by every means to avoid naming names. Since I wish to point out the fruitful tendencies of a future art of painting, I must deny the support of my hope from the many who in reality deserve mister Corinth's strictures. Doubtless I need not say that I exclusively mean honest and energetic workers, personalities who concentrate their creative will in a totally new way and much more intensely than mister Corinth ever has. Of the foreigners we have Matisse and Picasso, de Vlaminck and Kees van Dongen. Among the Germans, Pechstein and Purrmann,[2] Erbslöh[3] and Levy[4], Kirchner, Heckel and Schmidt-Rottluff. There are certainly a few names missing, but I assume gladly and joyfully that none of them has ever visited mister Corinth's academy.

In Impressionism, the world as human representation seems not only to be drawn into the uncertainty of movement, but this representation is itself also dissolved in an eternally flowing play of elements. There was no certainty, nothing absolute in either object or subject. The whole of existence was dissolved in a dream which could only be quickly perceived and reproduced.

As a matter of fact, Impressionist art was founded not on representation, if one understands this to be the joining of several impressions into a clear picture in the memory, but on perception (like perhaps every naturalism). This new kind of perception was brought into being by the artist's devotion to nature, his empathy with her cosmic life. This plunged him into intoxication and moved him to paint it in all its manifoldness with every means that his palette could provide. Gradually, however, this way of seeing became habitual, the devotion to nature and the recording of visual perceptions no longer exhausted the artist's powers of creation. The artistic will seeks a new task, which it naturally must find in the development of the new naturalism; it is to stabilise a naturalised individuation on a personal basis, to make the stimulus necessary by abstracting it from the incidental.

Personal sensation was the foundation of creative power, something that was spiritual and therefore moved, and something subjectively arbitrary. On this basis the personal rhythm of sensation was not restrained by the natural organic form, which was indeed excluded *a priori*. And when this rhythm wanted to take this new colour-world of cosmic becoming which had been won from nature, were not the gates thrown open to every arbitrariness, to an artistic anarchy? Art was never simply subjective arbitrariness, but rather a tension between the artistic subject and a somehow objective obstacle which artistic will made for itself. The new ideal is: the picture. Once again one wanted to create a structure independent in itself, free from all alien, outward connections. No longer was it nature but the picture that was the regulative hindrance which dictated the laws of creation to the artist.

The difference between every Expressionism and every Naturalism lies in the will to create.

'Sculpture and painting are, in contrast to architecture, called imitative arts. This name expresses the difference only and disregards what they have in common.'

'As long as it has to do with imitation, there is something in the visual arts of natural research, and artistic activity is tied to this. The problems of form which are presented to the artist in this way come from nature, are dictated by perception. If these problems alone are solved, i.e. if what is created exists in this connection only, then it has as a structure not attained to any independent totality that can stand up for itself in comparison with nature. In order to attain to this, its imitative content must be developed towards the higher region of art from a further point of view which I would like, generally speaking, to refer to as the *architectonic* one; here, naturally, I wish to leave aside the usual special meaning of this word architecture. This word I understand then only as the construction of a formal whole, independently of the formal language. A drama, a symphony have this architecture; this internal construction is an organic totality of relationships, just like a picture, a statue, even though the different arts live in completely different worlds of form.'

'The problems of form which arise with this architectonic creation of a work of art are by no means self-evident ones, presented directly by nature; they are, however, the absolutely artistic ones. Architectonic creation is that which makes a higher work of art out of artistic natural research. That which we call imitative represents a world of form taken from nature herself which, in order to become a full work of art, must first be worked upon architectonically. In this way sculpture and painting first enter that sphere common to all the arts, from the world of mere naturalism enter the world of true art.' (Hildebrand: *The Problem of Form*).[5]

Hildebrand's formula of 'architectonic creation' embraces the Expressionists' will also, but on a completely different basis. The fundamental differences between a sculpture of Hildebrand's and one of Matisse's is explained by Rodin's life's work. The manner of his impressionistic naturalism must constitute the basis for every future fruitful development. The assertion that Impressionism constitutes an end-phase is just a phrase. It is a beginning, for it is the body of evidence for a new art, much as was the naturalism of the Quattrocento for classical art. This new point of view, won from the cosmic, this will to the phenomenon, deserves to be clarified and stabilised. Behind fleeting appearances Hildebrand still searches for the 'thing in itself', behind the cheats of perception, the clarified form and lucid space, he is a classicist. But for the modern artist the absolute is no longer to be sought behind the relative, but rather the relative must be transformed into clarity and necessity. For the modern artist nothing objective can constitute the creative point of view, since he knows with the sureness of experience that there is no objective certainty. He can be led by his personal sensation alone. But its peculiarity is always to emerge anew from the contact with the object, i.e. not to stylise, but to will a style. The world of forms does not exist *a priori* or does not force the objects into shape, but rather comes into being every time out of the tension between subject and object. It is not scheme but formation.

This will to formation will (without departing from the essential foundations) vary the basis which Impressionism created for it, and will eventually produce a new perception of nature. But it will be hard to discern here what was viewed differently from the outset and what must be attributed to the transformation of the impression. Artistic work is a simultaneity of reception, re-working and representation, so that it cannot be decided how much is to be attributed to the age, the intellect, or the hand.

The fundamental differences are: more clarity and simplicity, more expression, more of what is personal.

If I had to distinguish the tendencies of the Expressionists from those of their predecessors, I would say: Impressionist art is based on a qualitatively new and thoroughly differentiated perception of a new, that is of the cosmic object, a perception which had become an empathetic penetration of it. The expressive language which is the vehicle of this perception must have a mobile form. The Expressionists, however, mistrust the impression – immediate, multifarious in its chance nature – and seek to raise it to an unambiguous, clear, simple and necessary concept. Their work is based on abstraction and their language of form became an immobile one. Impressionism was nature research in a new direction inasmuch as one made the movement of the atmosphere into the point of departure for artistic work. One saw develop a 'recherche pédantesque des sensations rares' (Jules Lemaître)[6], a piling-up of new optical evidence of nature. But one left it to one's successors to create independent art forms on this basis, to form this perception into closed pictures.

From this one can understand the artists' inclination and the way in which they were influenced by certain primitive works and by certain other over-refined ones, such as those of the Byzantines. They found the same abstraction in both. A young German artist once said to me as he was looking at early Christian and Byzantine pictures: we must regard that as our highest goal, but we dare not use it. Hence another art's valuable influence is limited in its field of action. They can be strengthened in their aim of approximating to abstraction, but they may not adopt these forms. German artists suffer most from this. But this is no reason to cry blue murder about their abilities. One seeks, for example, a new movement. That of Impressionism, with its spreading, open continuity, is unacceptable to a will that aims at closedness of picture.

Our present-day world is truly not rich in expressive demeanour. One helps oneself here at first with descriptions of primitive behaviour, certain straddling positions of the legs and sharp angles made by the arms. This is not the highest originality, but neither is it awkward childishness. Behind whatever borrowings made from savage people's implements lies an eminent ability to re-experience those simple and expressive forms. For the artist, they are the adequate form of his imaginative content and not pure copies. That in this case it is another art form and not nature directly that influences Expressionism could only be taken for a symptom of decay by so weak-witted a naturalistic criticism as our own. Or was the Renaissance not the influencing of the existing naturalist elements by an art form older but adequate to artistic will? Such an influencing will always be in evidence when a creative will wrenches itself free of nature and, conscious of its power, presses on to create what is necessary, what has a life of its own. In view of the extent of such facts in the history of art one cannot deny the justness of these influences. The imitation of nature is actually not the constituent mark of visual art.

I cannot describe the differences from Impressionism or the peculiarity of the young art in more detail. I must refer the curious to my book on Expressionism, which will appear as soon as a publisher finds the courage to print it. Or, to speak in the language of Mr Corinth: when in the future a benign providence takes the trouble. This phrase is far too pretty in your mouth, Mr Corinth. You are providence for so many young artists, but your benignity consists in throwing them on the street and your taking trouble in doing just that to ensure that these artists provide us with pleasure as much as possible against your will. Your gentle care consists in writing empty phrases about things pregnant with possibility and your providence in calling an army of kitsch-painters Expressionists. We, friends of the new art, can do without the kitsch painters Manguin and Friesz, the adulterators of our ideals, and would like to see a few others where they are at home: in the Lehrter Bahnhof.[7] We want to see: Matisse and Picasso, de Vlaminck and Kees van Dongen, Pechstein and Purrmann, Erbslöh and Levy, Kirchner and Heckel, Schmidt-Rottluff.

Originally published as: M.R. Schönlank, "Der Expressionismus", in: *Nord und Süd*, XXXV, vol. 138, H.437 (1st September issue, 1911), pp.360–365.

NOTES

1. Lovis Corinth: "Die neueste Malerei", in: *Pan*, I, 13 (1 May, 1911), pp. 432-437 (p.434).

2. Hans Marsilius Purrmann: Speyer, 1880 – Basel, 1966. Painter, graphic artist.

3. Adolf Erbslöh: New York, 1881 – Icking, 1947. Painter, graphic artist. Founding member of the Neuen Künstlervereinigung München, from which later Der Blaue Reiter would emerge.

4. Rudolf Levy: Stettin, 1875 – 1944. Died while on transport to the concentration camp Dachau. Expressionist painter.

5. Adolf von Hildebrand (Marburg, 1847 – Munich, 1921. Sculptor), *Das problem der Form in der bildenden Kunst*, 3rd ed. (Strasbourg: Heitz & Mündel, 1908), pp.vii–ix.

6. 'A pedantic research into rare feelings.' Jules Lemaître: Vennecy, Loiret, 1853 – Travers, Loiret, 1914. Critic, dramatist.

7. See note 7 on page 112.

HENRI BERGSON'S WRITINGS

Henri Bergson[1], *Time and Freedom*[2]; *Introduction to Metaphysics*[3]; *Matter and Memory*.[4] Published as *Zeit und Freiheit*; *Einführung in die Metaphysik*; *Materie und Gedächtnis*. Eugen Diederichs, Jena.

To anyone who wants to work his way into its territory, philosophy will seem an inextricable chaos in which the pettiest snatching at originality has, in its wretched longing for differentiation, apparently sealed up the few great problems which have moved humanity since the earliest times with an abundance of solutions. Thus the kingly science which, according to Simmel, signifies a reaction to the totality of existence, has become a confusion which must be penetrated by the breath of a creator, so that the waters will part and a division be made between heaven, water, and earth.

One such artist is Henri Bergson. I see him stepping up with his chisel to the block and splitting it up, working two figures out of the dead stone and then rejecting them in order to come close to the *genius loci* between them. 'If one stuck literally to what metaphysicians and scholars say, and likewise to the content of what they do, one could believe that the former have dug a deep tunnel under reality and the latter have built a beautiful bridge across it, but that the living stream of things slips through between these two elaborate constructions without touching them.'[5]

To comprehend this stream, Bergson for his part re-examines the means of perception. How highly are we to estimate concept and thought? They acquire their value from practise, says Bergson, and since practical action finds it convenient for the grasping and conquest of phenomena, our intellect mechanises events. The actuality of the intellect is always interested either towards a goal or from a point of view and it will not do to apply this particular way of doing things to the disinterested apprehension of the object. And then: every analysis opposes us to the things, tears open a rift between subject and object that cannot be bridged by the concept, 'since it is a schematisation, a simplified reconstruction, often a mere symbol, and in every case a mere *view* of reality flowing away.'[6]

In order to capture the eternally emerging continuity of life, the untiring creation of the new, Bergson must find a new means of perception. It is intuition by means of which we see things, so to speak, from within; a kind of intellectual discovery by empathy which signifies a meeting, a coinciding with the object, so that I now possess its innermost life, its most individual, inexpressible essence. Whereas the understanding breaks down every event into its parts and vainly seeks to reconstruct the true movement and continuity by means of stable elements, instinct goes straight to life itself and finds here, not calm, limit and space, but movement, flowing away and time.

I think this has been the cataclysmic experience for Bergson, after his more artistic attitude to the external world had pointed to the means of perception of intuition: that everything is eternal flow, blurring of distinctions, and becoming. It is the starkest contrast if we set Bergson against the philosophy of antiquity. Its essence is exhausted in the development of that which is unalterable, of the immoveable, eternal ideas. Only by the fact that one had made a principle of that which persists, of existence resting in itself, could Zeno have denied motion in his famous paradox, whereas he had in fact only made it into an extent of space. Christian philosophy and science, too, are spatially oriented, and even modern science emphasises 'the identity of the world with itself'. Its 'laws' deny the possibility of anything new in the world.

What is Bergson's '*durée intérieure*'? It is the immediately living time as the unfolding of life, an uninterrupted, seamless coherence, '*le progrès continu du passé*'. It is not analysable and measurable – that is, based on false spatial analogies, against which Bergson is on his guard. It is an absolute irreducible, simple and clear fact, and immobility is just the outer limit of the slowing-down of the movement, a limit perhaps only imagined, one never realised in nature. This *durée* is not to be grasped by analysis; one must put oneself into it by intuition in order to achieve that tension which we can pursue from two sides. On one side we meet 'an ever more dispersed duration (…), the pulse of which is faster than our own, hence divides our simple perception and thins down its quality into quantity: at the limit would be the purely homogenous, the pure *repetition* by which we define materiality. In the other direction we approach a duration which becomes ever more tense and draws itself together, growing ever more intense; at the limit would be the eternity (of life).'⁷

Thus Bergson comes from the definition of duration to the great problem: matter and mind, and devotes his book *Matter and Memory* to its solution. His concept must have more application to psychology than to any other field. Here everything is continuous becoming. First he opens the rift and places matter at one end of *mood*, and *mind* at the other. But the first has only come into being through the intensification of the second. He seeks to make this clear in one of his most vivid and magnificent images. The poet can produce a new poem by inspiration, but if the creative tension relaxes at all the poem breaks down into letters and words automatically, so to speak.

'The universe, the absolute itself, is emergence and life', a creatively formative impulse that ensouls matter, forms ever new and richer entities from it until the impulse frees itself in man and makes itself master of matter overcome. Thus we ourselves are waves in this rising flood; we stand in the front ranks of this upward-thrusting self-development and unfolding of the world; the great rising wave has reached its high point in us. But it itself presses forward, over and past us, we who are merely fleeting, ephemeral, unique materialisations of the inexhaustible rhythm of life. Since the universe itself lives and strives, we can only approach it when we direct our gaze to our living desire. It is not in thought that God lets himself be represented, he is no idea resting in itself, no pure form; he is movement, becoming, growth. There, in the free act of artistic imagination, he is present, there, in us, his act of creation is repeated. 'We cannot understand that a world of things can be created, but that our own doings grow and develop is a thing that every one of us can see in himself. This doing is the essence of the world.'

In these acutely characterising words of Richard Kroner (*Logos*, I)[8] we find the definite statement of Bergson's view of free will. A person who feels himself so eminently active, so creative in relation to the world as only an artist can, must oppose the depersonalisation and devaluation of life. Whereas all matter follows, must follow, unalterable, like laws, so that in its presence every future is calculable, man has the possibility of choice, or at least can have it. For freedom and necessity are only differences of degree. The more we take ourselves into possession, the more we are individual and personal, the more freely we will act. But it can happen that men have never once known true freedom from birth to death. So says Bergson in his first work *Time and Freedom,* a work of genius: 'There are two different selves, one of which is so to speak the outer record of the inner one, represents it spatially and to a certain extent emotionally. We attain to the inner one by a deep meditation that lets us perceive living beings in our inner states, which constantly transform themselves, beings that resist any measurement, interpenetrating each other totally, and whose sequence in time has nothing in common with a marshalling in homogeneous space. But the moments in which we apprehend ourselves in this fashion are rare and so we are only seldom free. Mostly we live alienated from our true self, we notice only the colourless ghost of our self, the shadow cast by pure duration in homogeneous space. So our existence unfolds itself more in space than in time; we live more for the external world than for ourselves, we are more acted on than acting; we speak more than we think. To act freely means once again to take possession of ourselves, to put ourselves back in pure duration'.[9]

I do not know if I have succeeded in indicating the wealth of acute problem-setting and highly individual solutions and in distancing this ample, creative spirit from the grocers and dairymen of present-day philosophy. It will not help at all in bringing him closer to us to emphasise where he is reminiscent of others. Even if we are reminded of Fichte and mysticism, of Mach and James, no division and synthesis of this kind will bring us closer to Bergson's thought-processes. Here, he would perhaps answer us that all of the present is a point which, saturated with the moments of the past, strives for the future. He wants to be seen as a whole, as an artist, as master of the world, as connoisseur of the material, as creator from the virgin soil. Once again he has given a significant answer to the whole, perhaps outside the limits of philosophy. But the limits are not there to cramp the mind, but to be set by it.

Originally published as: M.R. Schönlank, "Henri Bergsons Schriften", in: *Nord und Süd*, XXXV, vol. 138, H.438 (2nd September issue, 1911), pp.429–432.

NOTES

1 Henri Bergson: Paris, 1859 – Paris, 1941. Philosopher.

2 *Essais sur les données immédiates de la conscience* (1889). Published in German as *Zeit und Freiheit* (Jena: Diederichs, 1911).

3 *Introduction à la métaphysique*, 1903; Published in German as *Einführung in die Metaphysik* (Jena: Diederichs, 1909).

4 *Matière et mémoire. Essai sur la rélation du corps à l'esprit* (1896); Published

in German as *Materie und Gedächtnis* (Jena: Diederichs, 1908).

5 Henri Bergson, *Einführung in die Metaphysik* (Jena: Diederichs, 1909), p.50.

6 *Op.cit.*, p.29. Bergson's emphasis.

7 *Op.cit.*, p.39., Bergson's insertion.

8 Richard Kroner, "Henri Bergson", in: *Logos*, 1 (1910/1911), pp.125–150.

9 Henri Bergson, *Zeit und Freiheit* (Jena: Diederichs, 1911), p.181f.

PAINTING AND PERSONALITY

If, in the course of determining the essence of the work of art, one seeks a characteristic common to them all, the first thing one must say is that they are all human productions, hence that their secret and their deepest essence, their very mark of identity lies in the personality. The world of objects, the sphere of existence belongs to all men in the same way, in any event it could belong to them in the same way; thus the difference, the nuance in the reaction to it, is what is most individual in a work of art. Its enigma and its greatness lie in the mystery of the artist's personality and not in the sphere of existence.

Taine[1] has tried to make us believe this in his *Philosophy of Art*. However greatly he has been tempted by the sciences and materialism, we can only regard the idolisation of merely influencing and conditioning elements as a vain attempt to eliminate the creative and to democratise art. It is the most delightful grace of a Frenchman and an illogicality unbelievable in its conceptual naiveté that leaps over a chasm like this: 'We managed to establish the rule that, in order properly to understand a work of art, an artist or a group of artists, one must imagine for oneself exactly the general intellectual conditions and the customs of the time to which they belong. There we find the ultimate explanation, there lies concealed the fundamental cause which determines everything else.'[2]

This proposition contains the same logical dualism which characterises the whole materialistic understanding of history. It is its distinction that it pointed out connections between series of events that had formerly been regarded as running on unconnectedly. The connecting together of all matters of cultural fact, from the economic to the intellectual, is its undeniable merit. But its most audacious hypothesis is that of matter as the cause of everything intellectual. Even if one cannot free the work of art from its background of the totality of life, this spirit of the age still did not produce the work of art, did not even perhaps produce the artist. For one would be equally justified in reversing the sequence of cause and effect and saying: the artist has produced the spirit of the age. Even if the artist is the product of elements which constitute his time, his work is an independent utterance of his mind, one which is only in a general way related materially and formally to nature, i.e. to the spirit of his age. That which connects with the other artists, with time, is the incidental aspect of his work. The unique, the personal, is his property; his work is spirit, creation, what is new and has never before existed. In the mystery of his act of creation art comes into being, his creative ability bridges the gap between nature and work, between chaos and the composed.

Nature, the spirit of the age do not give birth to the work of art and the picture is not parthenogenesis. One does not describe the birth of a new, a third, with impersonal expressions; not 'it' and 'one', but 'he': the artist.

If Taine quietly eliminated the artist and wrote a theory of values with little regard to personal, creative achievement, it fell to Mach[3] to annihilate the personality, which here had been left merely *hors de combat*, with the entire philosophical arsenal. In his "Analysis of the Sensations"[4] he poses the question: what is the 'I'?

'The I is past saving.'[5] It is only a name. It is only an illusion. It is an expedient which we need in practise, to order our ideas. There is nothing but connections between colours, tones, temperatures, pressures, spaces, times; attached to these connections are moods, feelings and wills. Everything is eternal change. If we speak of continuity or endurance, it is only because certain changes happen more slowly. The world is in a constant state of becoming, and by becoming it annihilates itself constantly. There is, however, nothing but this becoming. There is nothing beyond the coherence of colours, tones, and temperatures. Only in order to orient ourselves for the time being do we speak of 'I', of phenomenon and sensation, which, however, can never be separated but immediately flow into one another.

'The great gulf between physical and psychological research exists for the customary stereotyped way of seeing only. A colour is a physical object as soon as we, for example, take account of its dependence on the source of illumination (other colours, spaces). But if we take account of its dependence on the retina, then it is a psychological object, a sensation. It is not in the subject-matter, but in the direction of research, that the two areas differ (...).'[6] Thus perceptions as well as ideas, the will, the feelings, in short, the whole inner and outer world, forms itself out of a small number of similar elements with a degree of coherence varying constantly from the fleeting to the enduring. 'The whole inner and outer world, my "I" and that of the other, is just a heaving viscid mass that here becomes thicker, there seems to melt away. The "I" is only a name for the elements that are joined together in it.'[7]

'The elements form the "I". I sense green, is to say that the element green occurs in a certain complex of other elements (sensations, memories). When I cease to sense green, when I die, the elements then no longer occur in their customary easy association. There is nothing more to say. Only something ideal, stemming from the work of thought, has ceased to exist, no real or unified entity has. The "I" is no unalterable, definite, clear-cut unit. It does not depend on unalterability, on the definite capability of being distinguished from others, on sharp delimitation; for all these moments vary by themselves even in the individual life, and their alteration is even striven for by the individual. Only the continuity is important. It is, however, only a means to prepare and secure the content of the "I". This content and not the self is the principal matter (...). The "I" is irrecoverable. It is in some measure this insight, in some measure the fear it inspires, which leads to the most egregious, pessimistic and optimistic religions, ascetic and philosophical absurdities. One will not be able for long to close one's mind to this simple truth which has resulted from psychological analysis. One will then no longer be able to set such value on the "I", which varies even during the individual's life, and which can be partly or completely absent in sleep and when immersed in meditative contemplation, indeed just in the moments of greatest bliss.'[8] (After Bahr: *Dialogue of the Tragic*).

Hence the self is not a reality but a fiction, not a somehow enduring unity but the temporary product of flowing elements. What philosophy could be more adequate to Impressionism than this? It is extremely ingenious, in the current state of the development of psychology, to proceed from here to explain memory. But may one put to an Austrian professor of Physics and his enthusiastic disciple, the writer Bahr, this question: how is the artistic act of creation to be explained if the self is a unit only from the point of view of mental production? It seemed to me, too, that there were personalities in modern painting to which one could somehow draw near with this view alone. Does not van Gogh seem to be someone else in almost every one of his paintings? But I obscurely glimpsed the connections between the *Potato Eaters*[9] and the *Street of Arles*[10], moments which became ever clearer and more distinct. Today I am convinced that even this chameleon had something in his personality that remained the same through all the changes or, to put it better, that all his work was just the search for the most adequate means of expression of his personality. It was always the same 'he' who stood as creator behind all these so different appearances; a thousand things changed him or, better, helped him to develop himself. The 'I' is in fact a given, even if not an unalterable one. All inpourings of the outer world leave their mark on it or, better, all influences adequate to its being work it to the surface. If the 'I' were just a conglomerate of elements, then all men would be the same. The difference of all men, especially of their highest type, the artist, is the best proof that the personality has a given core which shapes itself on the given influences as if they were its resistances. And if the core which finally emerges no longer bears the least resemblance to the original confused spherical mass, it still would not have become what it is if the least point on the original surface had been different.

In the discussion of the critics of the day and of the public, this disregard for the personality found expression in the overvaluation of 'technique'. One could hear Stahl and Kunze speak of the application of paint, hence of purely artistic moments. That the public à la Stahl[11] and Kunze naturally has no relationship to art was proved most clearly by the sterility of all this talk. Nobody tried to write anything like a system of dealing with matter, something which would really have answered a need. Here I can give only a few hints:

First of all, matter has its proper material life, which comes before all intellectual shaping and is dependent on it.[12] It has its own density and intensity, its own weightiness. But then the particular spirit of artistic willing can, in association with nature, take control of matter and express itself through it directly, without detours. The result will be a spiritualisation of matter. Whereas it is, in its autonomous gravity, inaccessible to the human apprehension, after it has become permeated with mind it actually has a downright appeal for the human capacity for empathetic penetration. Better known is the relation of matter to particular materials, by which I mean not just the ability to express a certain material, e.g. silk, satin etc., but materiality in general, e.g. light, volume, moistness, desiccation, frost etc. Matter acquires a fourth means of expression through its relationship with the surface, as a decorative colour of particular size and in a particular place beside others so delineated.

The artist acquires his ability to achieve these expressive possibilities from the qualitative laws of matter, or from the quantitative rhythms which he imposes on it. It would appear that both these applicative possibilities stand in a regular relationship to the expressive possibilities.

But all in all one would do better to let the artist himself speak about matter. Matisse, naturally, is right: 'But the painter's idea may not be considered in detachment from his expressive means, for it is only of use insofar as it is supported by means which must be all the more complete (...) the deeper his thought is. I cannot make a distinction between the feelings I have from life and the manner in which I translate these feelings into painting.'[13] But the layman has too often believed that the painter's idea exhausts itself in the brushstroke. The technique, too, is not the secret of art. It is the personality.

Hence we have the twofold question whether we have the scientific methodology conceptually to capture the personality and the desired painterly sensation? In principle: no. Language cannot distinguish the peculiarity of personality sufficiently.

'L'*individualité* des choses et des êtres nous échappe toutes les fois qui'il ne nous est matériellement utile de l'apercevoir. Et là même où nous la remarquons (comme lorsque nous distinguons un homme d'un autre homme), ce n'est pas l'individualité même que notre oeil saisit, c'est-a-dire une certaine harmonie tout à fait originale des formes et des couleurs, mais seulement un ou deux traits qui faciliteront la reconnaissance pratique' (Bergson, *Le Rire*).[14]

The painterly sensation, too, lies outside the literary, outside indeed the language of ideas. The most convincing proof is direct experience, more convincing for me than all the statements of artists or the acute case made by Fiedler[15] in his essay "The Origin of Artistic Activity",[16] which might convince even the top-loftiest intellectual. And finally: who would paint, if his need to express himself could be fulfilled with words?

If it is, after all, impossible in principle to fix the essence of personal painterly sensation in words, there may still be ways to approach it. For me, one of them might consist in the retracing of the artistic process of creation. This way calls for the drawing of the direct instinctive experience into consciousness. If I retrace the artist's work step by step, it should be true that no trait of the personality or of the unique sensation of the painter will escape me. Thus the first requirement would be a psychology of artistic creation. But I do not delude myself about the ultimate value of this method either. 'I could tell you how I started working on this picture, what I did next and what I painted later, but what use would this sequence of events be? *Ce sont les émotions qui font l'art et sur les émotions on ne peut dire rien*', said Matisse to me. And then: any conceptual formulation would have to tear itself into a profusion of moments, to divide into a temporal sequence that which in reality is a coherent and almost simultaneous event.

The other way consists in tracing the created forms back to their fundamental mathematical forms, to freeze them, as it were. There is a measurable stretch from the inorganic, geometrical form to the shaped, living one, a stretch on the basis of which one conceptually can express the individual peculiarity. The young Goethe declared this in Erwin von Steinbach, but at the same time he qualified this method as leading only to the threshold of the mystery. And he also drew the conclusion that one all too often would like to lay at the door of the modern public:

'Now this characteristic art is the only true one. If it produces its effect from inward, unified, personal, independent feeling, unconcerned with, indeed unconscious of everything outside, if it is born of the wildest crudity or the most cultivated sensibility, it will be whole and living. You will see countless degrees of this in nations and individual men. The more the soul is elevated to a feeling for propositions, which alone are beautiful and eternal, the principal harmonies of which can be *demonstrated*, but the mysteries of which one can only *feel*, and in which alone the life of the god-like genius can frolic, the more this beauty penetrates the essence of a mind so that it seems to have been born with this beauty, so that nothing else seems to satisfy it, (...) the happier is the artist (...) the more deeply bowed we stand and worship the anointed God.'[17]

Originally published as: M.R. Schönlank, "Malerei und Persönlichkeit", in: *Die Aktion*, I, vol.31 (September 18, 1911), pp.974–979.

NOTES

1. Hippolyte Adolphe Taine: Vouzers, Ardennes, 1828 – Paris, 1893. Cultural critic, historian, philosopher.

2. Hippolyte Taine, *Philosophie der Kunst*, vol.1 (Leipzig: Diederichs, 1902), p.10. Originally published as *Philosophie de l'art* (Paris, 1882).

3. Ernst Mach: Brno, 1883 – Vaterstetten, 1916. Physicist, philosopher.

4. Ernst Mach, *Die Analyse der Empfindungen und das Verhältnis des Psychischen zum Physischen* (1886).

5. Ernst Mach, *Antimetaphysische Vorbemerkungen*, section 12. All Mach citations from: Hermann Bahr, "Das unrettbare Ich", in: *Dialog vom*

tragischen (Berlin: Fischer, 1904), pp.92ff.

6. Ernst Mach, *Antimetaphysische Vorbemerkungen*, section 9.

7. *Ut supra*, section 11.

8. *Ut supra*, section 12.

9. Vincent van Gogh. *The Potato Eaters*. 1885. Oil on canvas. 82 x 114. Van Gogh Museum, Amsterdam; *The Potato Eaters*. Oil on canvas. 73.9 x 95.2 cm. Rijksmuseum Kröller-Müller, Otterlo.

10. Raphael most likely means van Gogh's *The Road Menders in Saint-Rémy*. 1889. Oil on canvas. 71 x 93 cm. Washington, The Philips Collection (at the time in the possession of Hugo von Tschudi, Berlin); was shown in exhibitions; Raphael might have seen it as *Strassenbau in Arles*, in: Julius Meier-Graefe, *Vincent van Gogh* (Munich: Piper, 1910), p.33.

11. Fritz Stahl (real name Siegfried Lilienthal): Rosenberg, 1864 – Berlin, 1928. Art critic for the *Berliner Tageblatt*.

12. Raphael probably meant to say 'independent' here.

13. Henri Matisse, See note 1 on page 95.

14. Henri Bergson, *Le Rire. Essai sur la signification du comique* (Paris, 1910), chapter "Le comique de charactère." Raphael's emphasis.

15. Conrad Fiedler: Oederan, 1841 – Munich 1895. Art critic.

16. Conrad Fiedler, *Der Ursprung der künstlerischen Thätigkeit* (Leipzig: Hirzel, 1887).

17. Johann Wolfgang Goethe, "Von deutscher Baukunst" (1772), in: *Goethes Werke* (Hamburger Ausgabe), vol.12, edited by Erich Trunz (Munich, 1988), pp. 7–15 (p.13ff). Raphael's emphasis.

GOETHE'S BIRTHDAY IN WEIMAR

Weimar, this small, aristocratic residency. It is shortly before midnight, the last shops are closing. The whole place sleeps. We walk to the Goethe-Schiller monument and sit on the steps. The silence and darkness of the night force the whole confusion of thoughts together into a picture, an image, which through silence and darkness grows to immensity and then turns grotesque. The giant Goethe as the maker of a Table-Lay-Yourself, or the rich starry heavens as a bouquet of flowers on the Great Wain. Midnight strikes. We lay some flowers on the base of the monument and sit down again on the steps. Three men come out of the 'Werthersgarten' across the way. And with their racially-pure Germanic fully-loaded beer bellies they say that authentically Jewish word 'Meschugge'. They go by and all is quiet.

'If one had imagination one could this moment imagine a procession of people celebrating this man's birth.'

'If one had imagination: spectacles, frock-coats, dusty parchments.'

Next day the flowers had disappeared. Not put off, we lay down three times as many. But the previous ones were wreaths of stubble with the inscription: The flower kleptomaniacs, from considerations of cleanliness. Dedicated to Goethe's birthday, 1911.

Belvedere. Below us lies Weimar, nestling in the Thuringian countryside. The lines of the hills climb softly, charmingly, and extend clear over a wide area. Here the landscape breathes the same spirit of the familiar, which has become the *milieu* of culture below in the town. No city in Germany has this unitary culture. Everywhere the same love of all things, the gift of sinking into the whole of existence. As long as he lent the presence of his creative spirit to this circle of people, 'the gates and streets of Weimar really were open to every corner of the world.' But when he went, there was only a sentimental dilettantism that makes one feel physically sick even as one reads it.

What makes him into a giant out of this *milieu* was his gift of elevating the all-too-human into a universal human greatness.

'Then become a Neoclassicist!'

'Leave me in peace with all your Neos. But he could do one thing: create! Who of our painters and literati can still do this? Just look at these boring Kodak snaps in books and pictures, as if all artistic powers were bankrupt. The culture of Impressionism has made the formative mind into a fabulous creature, put out to grass on desert wastes. If it occurs to the odd person to call nature a goose, the amnesiacs send him to the paupers. Fortunately this is how they are by the grace of

God. When the photographers are dead they will surely rise, the shapers of our own existence – let's go to the theatre!'

'Are you not surprised at Goethe's theatrical tendencies?'

'Not at all. When the main thing in art is not the copy of nature by the grace of Donkey, but rather the creative gift of a shaper, then we can say: I have never viewed all my works and achievements other than simply symbolically, and it is all the same to me at bottom if I make pots or dishes.'

We were able to mime for a while in the Nature Theatre. Then we walked through the Poets' Paths.

'Perhaps the most important need is to become clear in one's mind about Goethe's limitations.'

'You should fear the spirit of Goethean philologists.'

'Let this gang of intellectual shopkeepers be. After all, you can see how these bloodless paupers celebrate the birthday of the master who feeds them. They would eat just as meekly from a filthy trough. Hebbel once marked out Goethe's limitations and found, 'that in Faust, having to choose between an immense perspective and a proscenium decorated with figures from the catechism, he preferred the painted boards and reduced the *birth-pangs* of a humanity struggling for a new form, which we rightly perceived in Part One to the pathological motifs of an individual cured by an arbitrary act, psychologically only barely justified (…)'[1]

'And how do you explain that?'

'Naturally by the essence of his character, the fundamental need of which was harmony. It was his nature to resolve every dissonance. The disharmony between the conscious personality and the universe cannot be resolved. Hence he could only avoid it. Neither was there a pre-established discrepancy in the legend of Dr. Faustus, as there was in that of the Wandering Jew, for example. Thus Goethe, with his reverent honesty and love for the object, could never make anything out of this material.'

'So you mean that a new giant must affirm the disharmony between the individual and the universe and from this affirmation to draw his life-energies, and from them to derive the new form of modern personal life.'

Below, in the town, superior daughters were patiently brought for walks. Our flowers had disappeared.

'You see, Goethe as bearer of German culture has become a farce *anno* 1911. I am going to make a journey to where the German forests are densest and the clerics blackest.'

'And German culture is there?'

'At its strongest – zero.'

Originally published as: M.R. Schönlank, "Goethes Geburtstag in Weimar", in: *Die Aktion*, I, vol.32 (September 25, 1911), pp.1006–1007.

NOTES

1. Friedrich Hebbel, introduction to *Maria Magdalena* (1844), in: *Werke in 2 Bdn.*, vol.2, ed. by Karl Pörnbacher (Munich: Hanser, 1952), p.284. Hebbel's emphasis.

PURRMANN AND LEVY

The crop which I could select in the Salons des artistes was scant and would be shameful in comparison to other countries, if German art had nothing more to show than here in Paris. But here, too, the Germans follow the total rhythm of the exhibition.

Whereas French painters are represented by Matisse only, and Picasso, Braque and Derain are missing entirely, the most gifted young Germans have stayed away for personal reasons and from sober principle. I wish to speak of these latter: first of all, about Purrmann and Levy.

Hans Purrmann was an artist who was already esteemed in Germany and acknowledged by the really authoritative critics. It was painters – hence connoisseurs – who bought his things in the Secession exhibitions. One loved the youthful strength in his pictures, which made one recognise the born painter, the instinctive insouciance which, in its giftedness, never missed the mark; one admired the fullness poured out by an undoubted talent. Even if the public was often stupefied, the connoisseurs wound their expectations to the highest pitch.

Purrmann, in his turn, realised that in this way he would come to husband his temperament, to give of himself and, in the happiest event, to supply more or less good painting all his life. He felt the need to secure firm and solid ground for his gifts, one on which they could work rationally and attain to an ever more perfect art. He oriented himself on the new efforts in French painting, which were concentrated around Matisse and were directed at achieving hue, character, and stability behind the fleeting charm which the Impressionists had produced with such admirable mastery. One wanted to fix, to condense, concentrate one's sensations; one cleaved more to Cézanne than to Renoir, one worked again with line, one drew again.

These tendencies seemed to Purrmann to contain the most fertile elements of style, they seemed adequate to his gifts and to the nature of his sensations. And with great self-discipline he reined in his power, in order to imbue the new principles with his spirit. What Purrmann produced in this epoch may have seemed timid to the admirers of his early works. But they underestimated the terrific services he did himself in this way. His works, once alive with youth, are restrained and disciplined in their power. They have become superior in colour and drawing, they collect and concentrate all that there is to say. The works are more thought through, they are more calculated, considered, willed. But behind this process of reassuring stands the same fresh strength as before, except that it is on a very solid basis.

I believe that Purrmann has his clear and constantly alert intellect to thank for the fact that he has steered clear of Matisse's influence on this path to concentrating his sensations. He has oriented himself on him, but he has never performed the flummery that can be noticed in the Salons of the 'indépendants'. He has much to thank him for, but he has always remained completely himself. He has done nothing more or nothing less than so many gifted German artists before him.

Much of what I have said about Purrmann I could repeat about Levy. In him, too, we find the striving to concentrate and stabilise the sensations, the search for the most appropriate means of expression. That two such intelligent artists are developing themselves on these new forms of style is the best proof of their fruitfulness and necessity. The spirit of the younger generation no longer has room enough between the relationships of nature to personality, of colour to colour, which Impressionism found sufficient for itself. The new sensation has made *one* new demand: the demand for a closed picture. Impressionism was the psychology of nature. One interpreted nature, with which the painted canvas never lost its relationship. One ordered everything in the section of nature in relation to reality and did not go to any more trouble about pictorial unity than to see that a total colour harmony came into being. This was founded on the Impressionist way of working, but it could not prevent the young artists from going beyond it. One no longer submitted one's spirit to nature to receive one's laws, but to the picture. One proceeded from the surface format on which one worked, and first and foremost wished to achieve an equilibrium of lines, colours, and tonalities. Thus the pictorial unity provided the laws of the division of the masses, the harmonisation, for the final sifting of tonal values. By so doing, one went a fair step back to the traditions, but did not leave the basis of modern sensibility. In short, one did not become in the least academic by taking up old and sound artistic demands; rather, one tried to create new pictures, a new equilibrium and division of the surface, just as the Impressionists had created a new view of nature. Levy, who has taken special pains in his still lifes to find a new equilibrium within the concentration of his sensations, a personal reconciliation of lines and tonal delicacies, finds himself on a good road. On every canvas one senses his giftedness and independent will, which strives ever further to emancipate itself from all influences.

It is a new strength to work and a new energy which lies in these artists. No more insane just going at it, where the artist himself never knows what is to come out of it, no painting *à la manière de...* which is as simple as it is meretricious and mindless. As layman one can scarcely evaluate this energy. One must add to this that, by their own choice, they have no contact whatsoever with the public.

P.S. This contribution was written in Paris in the spring, while at the same time the two artists were shown in Berlin (Salon Cassirer). The Berlin critics have, almost without exception, ignored or damned them.

Originally published as: M.R. Schönlank, "Purrmann und Levi [sic!]", in: *Der Sturm*, II, vol.84 (1st November issue, 1911), pp.671–672.

BERLIN EXHIBITIONS

The exhibition of Hodler's works in the Cassirer Salon has the merit of bringing together works from every period of the artist's production, the drawback that a recent five-figure composition is missing. With its aid, one could have discussed the most interesting question thrown up by this exhibition: what significance has Hodler for a painting of the future? For one is inclined, especially in academic circles, to rate this very highly, and one adduces the exhibitions of Swiss artists, which have been notably of a very high standard throughout. But this work offers no lesson outside of its national limitations. I believe it is much more likely that Hodler's language must remain a completely personal one, because it stylises and constructs a scheme. Stylisations however, cannot be the exhaustive language of an age, even when, in the hands of a great artist, they encompass an admirably wide and generalised area of factuality. It is Cézanne, not Hodler, who has shown the only way in which a new painting can develop, has indeed already developed. Without Cézanne, there would have been no possibility of any of the so-called Expressionism, which has everywhere developed with national characteristics, although without national limitations.

In order to penetrate Hodler's multifarious and confused *oeuvre*, one may distinguish between figure-compositions and nature studies. These form a thread throughout his whole life and demonstrate a willing devotion to the objects, an intense love for the smallest thing. At the same time they reveal, almost up to the last years, his feeling his way towards the most adequate means of expression. In the early days, a continual oscillation between pure tonal painting and sharp, indeed bizarre line-work. Later he approaches the Impressionist problematics of colour, without even attaining to a similar harmony. His colours stand side by side in hard-looking specks; each of which, one could say, is a single individual. He lacks any ability whatsoever in that region of transitions in which the Impressionists made their greatest discoveries. This lack is not just one of colourism but also in the handling of line, wherever it should express the meeting of two compositional members, the meshing of two functions (and this lack has its ultimate correspondence in the composition). It is just these studies which most clearly show Hodler's temperament, even if too strongly on the negative side. He has no sensibility, no exuberant, life-enhancing sexual feeling. Everything becomes homogenous in his hands; Hodler does not seem to possess that Impressionist power to individualise the object in the atmosphere. Against that he has occasionally tired in his landscapes to give more than a psychological interpretation of nature and to achieve a picture by (forcibly) stylised parallelisms on the horizontal axis. A grey strip of cloud is reflected in the lake. These horizontal stripes of colour, laid above each other in parallel correspondence, are completely unsuccessful attempts to obtain a picture directly from nature, i.e. a statement which demonstrates a more compelling and visible unity than the pure colour harmony of the Impressionists.

There, however, where in recent years Hodler has set himself in front of nature without pretensions, he seems to me to have produced his purest, most achieved works. A new feeling for mass and, corresponding to it, a heavy new line allows him to paint these summits in which he seems to have solved the so neglected problem of mountain painting.

When one thinks for a moment of the child's play that Monet made of solving this in the pictures he brought from Norway's High Range, one sees immediately how intensely subject-matter and artist interact here in Hodler.

One cannot esteem the significance of this uninterrupted study of nature highly enough.

It provides the artist with the basics for his abstractions of colour and line, something which is proved by a complete parallelism between composition and each particular stage of the nature study. It forms the foundations and background of his creation. These foundations, however, need the figure and its gesture as well as the possibility of a grouping ordered schematically, i.e. in parallel fashion.

The first work of this sort is 'dialogue intime'. In front of a hillscape which climbs to a high horizon, an over-slender, naked youth walks solemnly with arms raised on a rectangular, sandy path.[1] The idiosyncrasy of every one of Hodler's gestures lies in its relationship to the body, i.e. in its short distance from it. Dance movements aside, one could confirm a certain proportionality, to be found only in Hodler, between the degree to which the silhouette is closed up and the reach of the gesture. This panel is painted in a colour harmony stylised towards grey and finds its unity in this general toning-down of colour. For the structure of lines, no matter how consciously they seem to be placed to assist one another, has acquired no inevitability; indeed, the very detailed working out of the landscape does not result in an optical unity with the figure, in spite of the similarity of mood.

The next picture, *Spring*[2], is already dated fourteen years later. It differs in the pure, hard colours painted without any consideration for truthfulness to nature. I am inclined to believe that its literary quality is the most interesting thing about the picture, since Hodler has not succeeded in combining both figures into a unity. Not only do they fall asunder as a group, but certain individual details are formed so independently that they distract the eye from the whole. On the other hand, the literary element signifies a new and attractive contribution to the psychology of youth, of sexual awakening. This seems to me completely to characterise Hodler's work: that he fills a general concept with a new content adequate to our time with the aid of an extensive personal power of experience and seeks this through a variation within his composition of figures.

All that is missing here is a large composition, which would undoubtedly have shown us how far Hodler has come in the unification of the surface. But memory tells us with certainty: there has been no change in the basis of an imagination working in general concepts, of a temperament which is artificial and intellectual, one which does not create in a directly sensual way. These are Hodler's limits. And it shows us something else: the wide area which Hodler can bring into his stylisations, the breadth of his personality: this is his greatness.

I feel the need to stand back from this major artist by building up a collection of snippets, for I wish to speak of the juryless kitsch exhibition. It is a pity that this sensation has become anything more than a statistic of impotence and an opportunity for liberal critics to confess their hearts to ciphers and to 'principle'. I never knew the artists of the New Secession thought no more of themselves than to act as an advertisement for inability. I thought that, when one had the opportunity to exhibit, one would have character and dignity enough to be careful beside whom one hung the products of one's inner excitation. But since it has been told of one of these gentlemen why he showed his work in the juryless exhibition, I will retail it in the hope of thereby amply characterising this quality. By placing one's work beside absolute impotence, one counted on the 'good coming into its own', 'producing its effect by comparison.' Whoever uses such a foil to produce his effect must naturally make this rule: 'Dilettantism is a necessity.' I would be slow to accept him, but would like the addition: it is all the same whether one plays the dilettante *à la* Raffael, or *à la* Neo-Impressionism or even *à la* Expressionism.

One of the artists of the 'New Secession', Mr Melzer, had a group show at Keller & Reiner. His woodcuts are to me the pleasant part of his work; whereas I can never get rid of the feeling of emptiness from the pictures, in every one of his cuts I see a closed and self-willed achievement. The harmony of colours is highly attractive in its exquisite delicacy, while the linear structure betrays a powerfully intellectual will. And yet this is a gift for illustration, and the exhibition was a promise of work that one may joyfully await. But there would be no surer way of nipping it in the bud than by dragging him before the public as a finished artist.

The education to art of the emerging artist and the layman: this great problem is posed by the exhibition of work from Mr von Kunowski's[3] school. His efforts over many years have had as their aim the determination of the extent to which art can be learnt, once one has thoroughly gone into the traditional and the modern. This simultaneous taking up of the modern may well have lent the exhibition a certain freshness which one otherwise misses at student exhibitions. Nevertheless I am not convinced that one has fully succeeded in one's aim. I do not believe that there is an absolute and teachable craft that can be detached from what an artist has to say. As the artistic content varies so immediately do the means of expression, and there is no technique, no ability on this side of or beyond all willing. The methodology and the philosophy of artistic means are determined by art, and not the other way around. Thus I miss a truly convincing artistic talent among these students, and on the other hand I can point to the fact that the most gifted of our young painters are self-taught.

Against this, Mr Kunowski's efforts seem to me to be of great value for our visual education. Anyone who knows how many eyesores should be reckoned to the account of blind insensitivity, how difficult has been the progress of every education of the eye towards the sensuous perception of reality, will now joyfully welcome it as a necessity that one has at last addressed this question systematically. Within these limits one cannot praise this energetic work sufficiently, and it was a happy thought to render the possibilities of progress enduringly accessible by producing an example. In the book *Unsere Kunstschule* (which appeared with the publishing house of the Nationalstenographie Liegnitz, 1910), Kunowski husband and wife[4] have set down the results in words and pictures, and it is to be wished that this titanic work should bear fruit for the cultivation of the Germanic eye.

One could perhaps say that in no country have so many and such good attempts been made to clarify and elevate the sensuality of the eye. (One could regard this as proof of how little visual culture the German people possesses). To this I can add that ambitious publication by Eugen Diederichs (Jena) of a history of art in pictures in 25 volumes at 6 marks each, hence a publication accessible to the widest circles of 25x200 good photographs from the art of all ages and cultures. Hopefully the monumentality of such a publication will impose on the German people the self-evident duty of exploiting this material.

It has been the cancerous harm of every art history and writing on art that one used too many words that had no essential connection with the work; that one in fact simply spoke away without visual material. This sorry state of affairs has now been completely set to rights. What we find in the three volumes is, in part at least, almost perfect. By these I mean in the two volumes which Professor Heidrich[5] has selected and introduced. Here a connoisseur has extracted what is typical and an empathetic historian has clearly and simply said what is necessary for the understanding of the subject. I only wish that, with such division into details, considerations of the whole would come more to the fore. It is an unavoidable duty to provide some pictures of altars in order to illustrate the combination of architecture, sculpture, and painting. It is not enough merely to speak of it, since most readers have no mental picture corresponding to the words. But, all in all, these old Netherlandish and Old German paintings are perfect samples of the whole. The work of Professor Hamann,[6] on the other hand, seems to have been unsuccessful. In such a monumental publication it is individualistic, scholarly whim to devote to a period of barely thirty years a volume with two hundred illustrations. How then is one to put the painting of the years 1300-1600 into three volumes? And it was precisely Italian painting that should have been the university of visual education. Equally, I see the introduction as an impossibility for the layman, and the reduction of the pictures to a tiny size as the best means of causing confusion.

This is to say nothing against the publication as a whole, of which one can only wish that the enthusiastic participation of the public will prevent its grinding to a halt, and that competent scholars will step in to change certain elements in the plan. Thus I find it incomprehensible that one intends entirely to skip French sculpture, which was after all the highest flower of medieval culture and the mother of all Western schools of sculpture. A volume illustrating the developments of landscape painting would seem to me desirable, because this is the subject-matter of modern painting.

When I look back, I marvel at the great many sights which the new season has shown. I note also, in the Academy: the National Gallery's new acquisitions. In the Künstlerhaus: Berlin in the picture.

Originally published as: M.R. Schönlank, "Berliner Ausstellungen", in: *Nord und Süd*, XXXVI, vol. 139, H.442 (2nd November issue, 1911), pp. 260–264.

NOTES

1. Ferdinand Hodler. *Zweigespräch mit der Natur* [Dialogue with Nature]. Around 1884. Oil on canvas. Kunstmuseum Bern, Dep. of the Gottfried Heller-Stiftung.

2. Fedinand Hodler. *Der Frühling* [Spring]. 1901. Oil on canvas. Folkwang Museum, Essen.

3. Lothar von Kunowski: Ober-Wilkau, Schlesien, 1866 – 1966, Düsseldorf. Painter, graphic artist, art critic.

4. Gertrud von Kunowski: Bromberg, Prussia, 1877 – Schönau am Königssee, 1960. Painter.

5. Ernst Heidrich: Nakel, Prussia, 1880 – Dixmuiden (Belgium), 1914. Art historian.

6. Richard Hamann: 1879, Seehausen bei Oschersleben, Harz – Immestadt, Allgaü, 1961. Art historian.

ON MODERN PAINTING

Julius Meier-Graefe: *Cézanne*[1]; *van Gogh*.[2] E. H. du Quesne-van Gogh: *Persönliche Errinerungen an Vincent van Gogh*. ['Personal Recollections on Vincent van Gogh'].[3] Published by R. Piper & Cie., Munich.

In all areas of intellectual expression our age seems to have lost the sense of a work complete in itself, because the producers have mislaid the feeling for a harmony between object and subject. When it comes to scientific books, one produces either endlessly sedulous works which root among the objects and thereby swell to the point of unreadableness, or subjectivities devoid of orientation or fundament; views, opinions, but never perceptions. These works have the merit of being thoroughly agreeable reading, even if one is usually as wise at the end as at the beginning. If I say to Mr Meier-Graefe[4] that this is not the way to produce science, he would say to me that he is proud to be a non-academic; this then gives rise to the necessity of writing his books all over again. I am not being fair to the author, because I am judging him from a standpoint which he neither has adopted nor could adopt. His works contain all the merits with which one has credited him and, among the non-academic art historians, there is hardly an artist so literate.

But this does not stop one from quoting as a judgement the following entry (26 Nov., 1838) from Hebbel's diary: 'The book is full of brilliant *points of view*, but it is altogether more a work of daring imagination than of calm comprehension, and that is not appropriate to the concept of science. One really will not be indebted to this book any more than one is to the tree, the stones etc. which give rise to thoughts in us. These books are written more for the author than for the reader. They are painfully hard to grasp and characterise, having only a dream reality, one which for us is hardly a reality at all. What distinguishes their content from that of real dreams is the constant effort to break through the cloudiness of vision and to enter upon the firm ground of ideas.'[5]

There could well be a great need for the *Personal Recollections* as a gloss on the life of van Gogh. One notices in every line that this book has been written by a woman, and this sets the tone of its charm. I have long wondered why none of our playwrights has made a play out of this truly tragic material, the life, i.e. the sufferings, of van Gogh. He is the modern hero who consumes himself. A wholly vague yearning makes him search, change profession three times; then he becomes an artist. His art devours him and he cries out for life. That van Gogh came to the same conclusion as Ibsen's *Rubek*[6] should provoke thought. Madame du Quesne-van Gogh has written the idyll, so to speak, from which this tragedy grew. Now, however, a poet may write us this tragedy.

Originally published as: M.R. Schönlank, "Zur modernen Malerei", in: *Nord und Süd*, XXXVI, vol. 139, H.443–444 (1st and 2nd December issue, 1911), pp.437–438.

NOTES

1. Julius Meier-Graefe, *Paul Cézanne* (Munich: Piper, 1910).

2. Julius Meier-Graefe, *Vincent van Gogh* (Munich: Piper, 1910).

3. Elisabeth Huberta du Quesne-van Gogh, *Persönliche Erinnerungen an Vincent van Gogh* (Munich: Piper, 1911).

4. Alfred Julius Meier-Graefe: Resita (Romania), 1867 – Vevey (Switzerland), 1935. Art historian, writer.

5. Friedel Hebbel, *Tagebücher 1835-1843*, vol.1, ed. Karl Pörnbacher (Munich: DTV, 1984), p.248.

6. The sculptor prof. Arnold Rubek in Ibsen's last play, *Wenn wir Toten Erwachen* (originally published Copenhagen, 1899), in: *Sämtliche Werke*, vol.5 (Berlin: Fischer, 1907).

CHARLES DE COSTER, FLEMISH LEGENDS

Translated into German by Marie Lamping and Frau von Oppeln-Bronikowski. Published by Eugen Diederichs, Jena.[1]

Anyone who has seen this book with its excellent woodcut on the cover and, in fond recollection of the "Ulenspiegel",[2] picks it up eagerly, will not be disappointed if he bears in mind from the outset that the "Flemish Legends" were produced nine years earlier. They contain as it were a promise of the latter work. Here lie in embryo all the character traits and artistic capabilities that we admired and loved in that great epic of the Flemish people; here they begin to develop. The subjects, too, are taken principally from the glorious age of the agonising wars of liberation and portray the character of the Belgian people. It is just that here everything is divided among individual stories, following a recipe of Goethe's, according to which the young artist should deal only with minor themes. So, together with the "Ulenspiegel", these legends offer us the rare pleasure of seeing an artist attain to the full, clear and necessary ripening of his gifts. These gifts were such as to encompass only a limited sphere, but that to the fullest extent and in the purest accord. That is why its revival is a noble deed.

Originally published as: M.R. Schönlank, "Charles de Coster, Flämische Legenden", in: *Nord und Süd*, XXXVI, vol. 139, H.434–444 (1st and 2nd December issues), pp.444–445.

NOTES

1. Charles de Coster, *Légendes flamandes*, 1858.

2. I.e. *La légende et les aventures héroiques, joyeuses et glorieuses de Thyl Ulenspiegel et de Lamme Goedzak au pays de Flandres et ailleurs*, 1868.

> Vive la bagatelle!
> Swift

DEAR MR PECHSTEIN!

Paris, Place du Panthéon 11.

It's a pity that you have helped to promote the view, put about by uninformed dispatches, that the art and the significance of Picasso consist in his having thought up a new form in which to render the cubical. *One can make Cubism and Futurism with the intellect, but a picture of Picasso's is a vision.*

Cubism is an attempt by creatively impotent seekers after fame, who have learned to 'hawk and spit' from Picasso and now, with all the wretched poverty of a few external appearances, set newspapers and exhibitions in motion in order to drum up business by advertising themselves. Art's Americanism. One says to oneself: up till now I have painted Neo-Impressionism. That was no go, for one knew Signac. Now Picasso has got straight to the cube. Now perhaps it will go better. For Picasso does not exhibit, and if he really is as he has been presented to us I would insult him to death, I, Mr Metzinger.[1] That's how they all are. They approach the thing from the outside and are very ingenious but still are never able to find their way into the inner. You as an artist, however, know that only the shaping of the experience is art.

And that is *Futurism*: a national Italian affair. The idiocy of incapable nerves, worn out by centuries of culture, nerves which have been overwhelmed by the whole confusion of the modern world without ever finding a single inner organ with which to receive it. Thieving from everything, academism and the total caprice of ultimate creative impotence.

But Picasso is the creator of a new world. He has brought it out of himself as a woman does the fruit of her womb; through the enormous capacity to give birth and in the agony of struggle. It is ultimate interiority, the vision of the self's experience. And in every moment it emerges anew in growth, in the logic of its own possibilities. Its riches become immense. And those few who will perceive them will begin a new life.

Because something is the case in nature – the psychic experience, too, the inner sensation, is still nature as such – does not mean that it deserves to be painted in a picture.

The world of art is pure creation, the latter's degree of distancing from nature being quite indifferent – here Poussin and Corot are at the same stage. It comes into being through the spiritualisation of experience, the concentration of the individual sensations according to a law which governs them, and finally through that inner *élan* which no psychology and no aesthetics will ever explain to us. *Here art and metaphysics come into contact with each other.*

The shaping of the world is Picasso's work. Again, it is not the work of a pure intellect that, coldly calculating, joins form up to form and from the one discovers the necessity of the others, but rather the work of his very life, of the evolution of the creator who experiences ever more richly the possibilities immanent in every vision and gives them an ever more plastic form. To give the vision an ever richer and, at the same time, more closed plastic appearance, one in which there is no more arbitrariness, chance or whim – this is Picasso's masterful will. Think of Rodin's ink drawings, celebrated for the beautiful way in which the master let the ink run around the paper. Perhaps Picasso would say to this: that is cheating, art is forming, forming is necessity. His essentiality, his experience compel him to it. His creative ability had him find *one* means in the direct representation of the cubical. Really only one, Mr Pechstein. It is the cement in a building, built up as none other of the moderns has done it, free from the memory of tradition, free from anecdote, not just in the literary and painterly sense – for what is Winter Morning, 10 a.m. on the Seine etc. if not anecdote – but also from the anecdote of psychic experience…

We will have to study long before we understand his laws and the vast world which he subjects to them. We should go in awe on this road. For he is great and pure. Let us not speak of the cube, leave that to the uninformed criticism for use on bourgeois coffee-tables. Nor should we speak of tonal passages or *couleur*. *What would you say if I told you that Picasso has shown me his latest pictures, in which he has used pure blue and red as pure matter – not, mind you, the colour of Matisse, but pure matter in full strength?* Let us try like him to become master of the confusion of inner experience that presses into us and increases and coexists, equal in value, but deriving from itself the laws with which to rule it…

That is a little of what a picture of Picasso's says to me. Because he not only seeks the cube but builds a world, it may even sound moral. This is my firm conviction: *Picasso's art must have as a consequence a new aesthetics and a new view of life.* We have long had Impressionism coffined. To us younger ones it was stupid, frivolous, self-deception. We have the task of showing our world.

Let us construct it with all our powers and say nothing about the means. For our world is the main thing!

In long standing affection

your

M. R. Schönlank.

Originally published as: M.R. Schönlank, "Lieber Herr Pechstein!", in: *Pan*, II, vol.25 (May 9, 1912), pp.738–739.

NOTES

1. Jean Metzinger: Nantes, 1883 – Paris, 1956. Painter, art critic, co-author (with Albert Gleizes) of *Du cubisme*, 1912.

MAX PECHSTEIN

Here in the somewhat ungenerous rooms of the Salon Gurlitt, I have to think of a certain ploughed field. A man strides over the fresh earth with long steps, pulling out the seed and scattering it with short, tight movements into an unforeseeable future. A peasant woman follows one step behind him, blessing all silently. Beneath them the indifference of the clod, above them the whole uncertainty of the arch of heaven.

Pechstein's art is like this, laden with the whole heaviness of personal experiences of nature and casting primeval seeds of creative power into it. Here we have autumn in all its golden splendour and the eternal cadence of its death; here nothing can rise again. There is the sea in the rhythm of its movement, rolling waves perpetually, up and down. There, a man recovering his health, with the whole misery of pain and the awakened fear for his life. It lies in the nature of Pechstein's artistic gift that he translates every personal experience of mood into the most elementary means of expression of visual art, into figure. Sea and morning, autumn and dune become figure with unmistakable gesture. Figure grows from the landscape like trees, bush, and meadow. They are like sand, leaf, and water. And so they move like the eternal elements which have caused them to come into being in the artist's imagination.

He, for whom the wellspring of his art lies in the vivifying feeling of nature, must of necessity feel attracted by the task of portraiture. To render a completely definite psychic circumstance in its essence by a necessary rhythm on the surface, by the *one* possible rescuing of the surface, that is in fact Pechstein's strength. No one mines so deeply into man's being; no one can brave the depths and shallows of modern man as he does. Who could so have brought this modern lady dressed *à la* Gerson[1] to the canvas that we can still speak of Eve behind the whole trappings of the modern miss? Pechstein's portraits are able to say the last word about a person, this is why they are such astonishing likenesses.

How Pechstein has avoided illustration, while resorting to the human figure in its gesture in his efforts to lend his vitally-felt experiences the highest expressive power, will always remain a secret of his talent. Still, one can say that he descended deep into the elements and expanded them by examining and determining the expressive power of the individual line and colour, their combinations and masses, and that he ascended higher by reducing the total experience to basic mathematical form and thereby assuring it of a pictorial stability which we can well find in the tradition, but not in Impressionist modernity!

It would be a crude misunderstanding of Pechstein's will, if we were to call him a naturalist, a psychologist or a journalist. He is far removed from everything anecdotal in like measure. This is shown above all by his still lifes. Here everything was dead, matter, arbitrariness; the artist could freely show the meaning of his creative deed. We see how he represents the basic elements of art: the falling rhythm in the free division of the masses, the rising one in the closed composition, the stabilisation of the objects by their being forced into a parallelogram. And the objects themselves? There is an apple of which any painter could be proud. Not because a bird would like to pick it, or a little girl to eat it up, but because it is an apple. An apple, and not just a dead material splotch of colour. This is a cloth with ornaments, in which the ornament is dissolved by the plangency of tones and the whole invested with the vitality of matter. These dead things, too, gradually acquire life, and that is the meaning of Pechstein's entire art. Out of the experiences to make an art that is solid and alive. One that does not strike dead but creates, forms, constructs.

Thus Pechstein fulfils both of Cézanne's demands, those for a sensibility and a logic of one's own. He treads the hair-fine path between the cliffs of naturalism and of formalism. The banality of the merely real and the artiness necessarily attached to its reproduction have found in Germany their conqueror in him. Everything separates him from the previous generation. For him art is once again law, one which has indeed existed from the beginning, one to which one must approximate afresh, approximate only. This is why he loves old art. Not, as with the aesthete, to tickle the palate. Rather, for the sake of the laws that subsist in it, and which also must subsist in any new art if it wishes to present the spirit of history with more than still-births. But these laws are no mere formulae, nonchalantly to be satisfied by ignoring every difficulty thrown up by actual perceptions stemming from taste or foreknowledge, as formalists and aesthetes, these of the modern art business, would have us believe. No, they are born more of reality and in the reality of the artist's pure sensation. None of the new slogans of abstraction and childishly primitive simplicity touch on Pechstein's will. Not simplicity, but unity, not abstraction, but creation; a work of his says this quite clearly. And so there is also a clean division in his work between him and the formalists, with their doctrines of pure surface and pure colour, which are no less banal and foolish for being of a more recent date than the Impressionist doctrine of bright colours.

On this mountain-ridge surrounded by dizzying seductions, Pechstein is helped by his peasant character. I sow, I will reap. For life is bound to justify creation, giving birth, growth. Here is part of a letter which he sent to me (dating from the spring, as he had the blow-up with the Secession people, and Berlin flocked to the fairground drum of Futurist trickery):

> 'The devil take it, it can't harm me, for I'm working away in spite of everything and everybody... Any work in which there is anything of the life-energy of its creator has permanence, and sooner or later will arouse in the individual person the enjoyment of beauty which it did in him who made it; and what can one do, one paints regardless, because one must. Theory is good, but a machine in theory, on paper only, is not yet working, causes nothing. Lord God, how powerful a thing spring is; it chives, sends out shoots and pushes out its strength, the flowers emerge, unconcerned by the manure with which the ground is fertilised.'

That is Pechstein the man. And why should one not speak of him, since his work in this exhibition teaches us to make no division between life and art? There are two self-portraits there, which tell us of an important transformation in his life. The first, dated 1910, still shows us the *defiant* pose of the world-conqueror, who has not yet felt the hard reality in its insurmountableness. The second, from the end of 1912, shows the man who has taken on the brutal load of existence as a concrete certainty in all its weightiness.

His art has become an endless road, a task, a moral duty to his talents. A world of experiences lies between these two pictures. It separates him now radically from all aesthetes and formalists, who only ever regarded him with squinting suspicion. And it brings him closer to the harmony of his spiritual powers, which are after all the vital pre-condition of all creation. That feral hunt, greedily pouncing on every appearance of life, always active, gathering, bringing home the treasures of Croesus as if one had to pile up everything attractive in life for grandson and great-grandson, has given place in no small measure to the urge for order, elaboration, shaping.

The organisation of the whole experience has grown, all arbitrariness has been limited, hemmed-in. Now words divide: Yes and No, Good and Evil, True and False, Beautiful and Ugly, with a division harder and purer. Compromise becomes impossible, because it would mean the betrayal of life and art.

For this freer glimpse of the man and the artist we are grateful to his frescoes in the Yellow Villa by the forest. By creating for us here a completely new experience of space, he let us step back in a new way from his individual pictures. Thoroughly worked-out as they may be, they still signify only indications, preparations for a new deed.

He gave the Germans a new art. Will he be able with its help to revolutionise the moribund state of an asphyxiating art politics? We wish to help him on this path with the cry: give us walls for Max Pechstein!

Originally published as: M.R. Schönlank, "Max Pechstein", in: *Pan*, III, vol.21 (February 21, 1912), pp.492–495.

NOTES

1. Berlin fashion store.

BIBLIOGRAPHY

THE EARLY CRITICAL WRITINGS OF MAX RAPHAEL (1910-1913)

1910

-Max Raphael-Schönlanke, "Die Amerikanische Ausstellung", in: *März*, IV, 12 (Mid-June), pp.497–500.
-M.R. Schönlank, "Berliner Ausstellungen", in: *März*, IV, 15 (August, 2), pp.234–237.
-M.R. Schönlank, "Ein Manetbuch", in: *März*, IV, 18 (August, 2), pp.494-495.
-M.R. Schönlank, "Der Sonderbund in Düsseldorf", in: *Nord und Süd*, XXXV, vol. 135, H.2 (2nd October issue), pp.154–157.
-M.R. Schönlank, "Die Weltstadt Berlin", in: *Nord und Süd*, XXXV, vol. 135, H.6 (2nd December issue), pp.506–509.

1911

-M.R. Schönlank, "Ossip Dymow. Der Knabe Wlass", in: *Nord und Süd*, XXXV, vol. 136, H.422 (2nd January issue), pp.168.

-M.R. Schönlank, "Die neue Secession", in: *Katalog der Neuen Secession Berlin. 3. Ausstellung: Gemälde; Februar-April,* 1911 (Berlin: Baron, 1911).

-M.R. Schönlank, "Weiss und Schwarz", in: *Nord und Süd*, XXXV, vol. 136, H.423 (1st February issue), pp.241–244.

-M.R. Schönlank, "Akademie und neue Künstlervereinigung", in: *Der Sturm* (1911), vol.49 (February, 4), p.392.

-M.R. Schönlank, "Curt Herrmann: Der Kampf um den Stil", in: *Nord und Süd*, XXXV, vol. 136, H.424 (2nd February issue), pp.355.

-M.R. Schönlank, "Die neue Secession", in: *Nord und Süd*, XXXV, vol. 137, H.427 (1st April issue), pp.70–73.

-A.R. Schönlank [sic], "Die neue Malerei. Neue Secession", in: *Der Sturm* (1911), vol.58 (April, 8), pp.463–464.

-M.R. Schönlank, "Die 'Neue Secession' in Berlin", in: *Bildende Küstler*, I, vol.4 (April?), p.155-156.

-M.R. Schönlank, "Liebermanns barmherziger Samariter", in: *Nord und Süd*, XXXV, vol. 138, H.435 (1st August issue), pp.210–212.

-M.R. Schönlank, "Der Expressionismus", in: *Nord und Süd*, XXXV, vol. 138, H.437 (1st September issue), pp.360–365.

-M.R. Schönlank, "Henri Bergsons Schriften", in: *Nord und Süd*, XXXV, vol. 138, H.438 (2nd September issue), pp.429–432.

-M.R. Schönlank, "Malerei und Persönlichkeit", in: *Die Aktion*, I, vol.31, (September, 18), pp.974–979.

-M.R. Schönlank, "Goethes Geburtstag in Weimar", in: *Die Aktion*, I, vol.32 (September, 25), pp.1006–1007.

-M.R. Schönlank, "Purrmann und Levi [sic!]", in: *Der*

Sturm, II, vol.84 (1st November issue), pp.671–672.

-M.R. Schönlank, "Berliner Ausstellungen", in: *Nord und Süd*, XXXVI, vol. 139, H.442 (2nd November issue), pp. 260–264.

-M.R. Schönlank, "Zur modernen Malerei", in: *Nord und Süd*, XXXVI, vol. 139, H.443-444 (1st and 2nd December issue), pp.437–438.

-M.R. Schönlank, "Charles de Coster, Flämische Legenden", in: *Nord und Süd*, XXXVI, vol. 139, H.434-444 (1st and 2nd December issues), pp.444–445.

1912

-M.R. Schönlank, "Lieber Herr Pechstein!", in: *Pan*, II, vol.25 (May, 9), pp.738–739.

1913

-Max Raphael, *Von Monet zu Picasso. Grundzüge einer Ästhetik und Entwicklung der modernen Malerei* (Munich: Delphin Verlag, 1913).

-M.R. Schönlank, "Max Pechstein", in: *Pan*, III, vol.21 (February, 21), pp.492–495.

ACKNOWLEDGEMENTS

In 1994 John Conolly and Brendan O'Byrne worked with me on the first draft of this translation, and I thank them for meticulous and patient collaboration. This translation is still as much their work as mine. I thank November Editions in Amsterdam and the publisher Gijs van Koningsveld for his engagement with the Raphael project. To the Faculty of Architecture, Technical University, Delft, my thanks for their financial support for this project.

ALSO IN THIS SERIES

Carl Einstein, *Negro Sculpture*,
translated by Patrick Healy (2014).

Karl Kraus, *The Last Days of Mankind: A Tragedy in Five Acts*,
translated by Patrick Healy (2016).

Karl Kraus, *In These Great Times: Selected Writings*,
translated by Patrick Healy (2014).

Else Lasker-Schüler, *My Heart: A Novel of Love*,
translated by Sheldon Gilman and Robert Levine (2016).

Walter Rheiner, *Cocaine: Selected Writings*,
translated by Bradley Schmidt and
Gijs van Koningsveld (2014).

Albert Ehrenstein, *Tubutsch*,
translated by Gijs van Koningsveld
(forthcoming 2016).

www.ingramcontent.com/pod-product-compliance
Lightning Source LLC
Chambersburg PA
CBHW031626210526
45464CB00004B/1773